A Broken River Books original

Broken River Books
10765 SW Murdock LN
Apt. G6
Tigard, OR 97224

ISBN: 978-1-940885-21-6

Printed in the USA.

ON THE BLACK

ED DINGER

BROKEN RIVER BOOKS
PORTLAND, OR

For Crystal, Ava, and Elle,
with all my love.

1

It was not the first time Clay White held a warm gun in a jelly hand and noticed the faint odor of sulfur in the air. He would have hoped that at his age he could have given up the chase, settled into blissful dementia, and played out the string, but no, here it goes again. Another body. Another situation spun out of control. Boxes within boxes within boxes to remove, open, and remove. Even with a fully functioning brain it had been difficult to piece these things together. Yet, didn't it always come down to this? A dead guy on the deck. The details of a murder that occurred nearly half-a-century earlier elbowed aside the facts of the tragedy that had just taken place; a killing, judging by the lingering smoke in the air.

Clay tried to focus on the body at his feet. "I don't understand." He addressed the crosshatch grip of the pistol he held loosely palm up.

"Are we going to go through this again?"

Clay turned to see a young woman standing in the entrance to the narrow slot in the room that afforded a kitchenette and provided a glimpse of the bathroom down a short hallway where the body lay. She was nicely turned out. Longhaired and leggy.

"Who are you?" he asked.

"Look in the right-side pocket of your jacket."

Clay slipped a hand into his windbreaker pocket and felt a thin slip of paper, the edge of which clung to his fingers. He pulled out a yellow two-by-two Post-It Note. On it was scrawled, "She's your granddaughter. Vivian."

"You wrote that five minutes ago," she said.

Well, if this was Clay's granddaughter, and there was every reason—and no reason—to believe it was, Clay pegged her as a calmer sort than her grandmother. Or maybe a better actress. Clay was the one who broke the tragic news to Grandma about her first husband.

"It can't be true," his soon-to-be wife murmured, head in hands.

"Save it for the second show." Clay walked to the bar to pour them both a drink.

Sipping whiskey and water, she slowly composed herself. "Oh, Clay. You didn't. Did you?"

This girl in the hotel room in the here and now would not require spirits or smelling salts. A dead body on the floor? No biggie.

"Were you the one who plugged the guy?" Clay asked.

"No. And let me guess. You don't remember who he is, either. Look in the other pocket."

In the pocket on the opposite side of his jacket, Clay found another sticky note with a single word written on it. "Barrett."

"That's Barrett?"

"That was Barrett."

Barrett, or whoever he was, came well dressed for a victim. A tailored suit and shoes cobbled from buttery, paper-thin leather. Looked to be thirty-five years of age or so. What a shame to check out so early. This Barrett had so many years of frustration, pain, and regret to look forward to. Not to mention confusion.

"It's too late for the speed wagon, and we don't need the cops just yet. Not until I have a chance to clear my head and sort things out."

"Clear your head? I don't think so, Grandpa."

"I need to get a handle on things. For my own sake, if nothing else."

"What's there to sort out? You shot him."

"Did you see it?"

"No, I did not see it. I didn't even know you were here. I went out to get some ice. The machine's not working on this floor so I had to go down a flight. And another. This place is still a dump. Like I've told you three times already, I was gone for a while."

"Did you hear the shot?"

"I think I can make an educated guess. Grandpa, you've never been this far gone. I know it's a shock and everything, but come on."

"Okay, just give me the skinny on the shooting."

"Promise you'll try hard to remember this time? And put the notes back where you found them. Just in case."

Clay returned the sticky notes to his jacket pockets.

"Okay," Vivian said. "It probably happened not even fifteen minutes ago. I called the police. Well, 911, anyway. I just said there had been an accident at the

Hotel Windsor. I didn't give them the room number. I had to call in something. If I didn't, somebody else would have. That's the long and short of it."

"I think I remember holding a gun. But I don't think I shot anybody. If I did shoot him, why? And where the hell are we?"

"I am standing in a junior suite at the Hotel Windsor, Center City Philadelphia. Where you are I have no clue. I thought you were home watching baseball."

Wasn't this the extended-stay place near the museum? Didn't she live here for a couple months when her apartment lease fell through just before her freshman year at Penn? Clay had helped her move. He now asked why she moved back to this "dump," as she called it.

"This is Barrett's room." She adopted a more sympathetic tone, reached out for his hand, and led him around the corner to a Lazy Boy. The arms of the fake leather chair were plastered with sticky notes. On a side table were several Post-It pads, a discarded cellophane wrapper, and a ballpoint. Clay sat down, still gripping the gun but resting it on his lap.

"I know you're confused, Grandpa. I know you can't help it. You can write all the hints to yourself you want, but sorting things out is just not going to happen with you going in and out of these states."

"I can't accept this as just one of those things. When somebody kills your partner, you have to do something."

"What partner? Do you see what I mean?"

"A man should at least know his role in something like this."

"It was an accident, okay? The gun just went off. Maybe you thought you were helping me. Maybe that's why you showed up out of the blue."

"Help you how? What are you doing here? What was he doing here? Why am I holding a gun? I need to know."

"Yeah, well maybe you're better off staying in the dark."

"So you do know more."

"Nothing that's relevant."

"Was this Barrett character blackmailing you?"

"In a way, maybe he was. I was hoping we could reach an understanding. Over drinks without lawyers."

"Were you two having an affair?"

"Barrett is gay. Was gay. Will you just stop it. The police are on their way, Grandpa. Whenever they show up we'll just tell them it was all an accident. Barrett was fooling around with this Goddamn gun and it went off and you didn't know better and picked it up."

"He shot himself straight between the eyes?"

"That's right. And leave blackmail out of it."

"Then what is this all about?"

"None of anybody's business. Certainly not the police."

"You know more than you're telling."

"Will you please stop it. This is not one of your old cases. If you ever were a private detective. The world has changed a lot since your day. Now private investigators work computers. I read all about it on the internet. They don't pack guns or shadow people or take jobs from mysterious blondes. They do database searches to get the scoop on some no-good in-law. When they do

5

get out of the office, it's to look for knock-off handbags. Maybe they make sure the guy who filed an insurance claim really does have a bad back. Or they track down elderly grandparents who wander from their homes or the hospital. Loving, wonderful, but disoriented grandparents."

"Maybe they could also tell me why I'm holding a gun or why there's a dead body in the bathroom."

"Yeah, maybe in a perfect world we'd know everything in the end."

"But what about this world? What about the snuffed candle in the other room? What about you and me and this cold, black piece of steel? Are you going to lay it out before the blue boys show or are you going to keep playing me for a sap?"

"There you go again. Talking like some old black and white movie."

"Maybe I'm not as far gone as you think." Clay got to his feet, stuffed the gun in his waistband, and smiled. "Maybe acting a little off in the head is good for business. We're talking blackmail. Then we're not. All I know, sister, is you keep trying to pull the fast one on me."

"Whatever. I'm making coffee while we wait for the police. You want some?" The girl turned to walk away.

"How do I even know you are my granddaughter?"

"How do you even know who you are?"

Clay sat down again in the Lazy Boy. He glanced at one of the notes stuck to the arm of the chair. "Bettendorf." He peeled off another one that read, "Who won the game?" He reached over to the side table for a Post-It pad, took up the ballpoint, and wrote, "Focus." He pulled the square off the pad and looked for an open spot on the chair arm to place it. Another note caught his attention. He peeled it off to read, "Focus."

Clay closed his eyes. How was he supposed to understand what was going on? A gun, a dead body, a blonde. And no clue. He took a deep breath, opened his eyes, and across the room saw a Post-It Note stuck to a mirror. On it was written "Dry Cleaning." Had he forgotten his dry cleaning? He must have forgotten to pick up his dry cleaning. What time was it? It was dark outside. The cleaners was probably about to close and he hadn't picked up his dry cleaning. How could he be so stupid? Where had the time gone? He had to hurry if he was going to get to the cleaners before it closed.

Clay pushed himself out of the chair and rushed to the door, but as he passed a hallway, something caught his eye. Some guy's legs were sticking out of the bathroom. Slowly Clay walked down the hallway. Something was terribly wrong. He stepped closer until he could see inside the bathroom. There was blood pooling on the floor. Whoever it was had been shot in the head. That's when Clay noticed the all-too-familiar odor of ignited gunpowder. He looked down at his waistband and pulled out a warm gun.

"I don't understand." He turned his hand to inspect the crosshatch grip of the pistol.

"Jesus Christ, Grandpa! Not again!"

Clay turned to see a young woman standing in the entrance to the narrow slot in the room that afforded a kitchenette and provided a glimpse of the bathroom down a short hall. She was nicely turned out, longhaired and leggy, holding a jar of instant coffee.

"Who are you?" he asked.

The girl sighed. "Look in the right pocket of your jacket."

Clay slipped a hand into his windbreaker pocket and felt a thin slip of paper, the edge of which clung to his fingers. He pulled out a yellow two-by-two Post-It Note. On it was scrawled, "She's your granddaughter. Vivian."

A minute later Vivian led Clay to the Lazy Boy and made him sit down.

"What about the dry cleaning?" he asked.

"You don't need to worry about that." Vivian removed the reminder from the mirror. "Barrett doesn't need to worry about it anymore, either."

"Do you think he has any coffee?"

She held up a jar of freeze-dried Folgers. "Yes, I think he just might. You want some?"

While Vivian returned to the kitchenette to finish making the coffee, Clay began to sort through the notes stuck to the arm of the chair. "Who won the game?" "Bettendorf." "Box top." "Stoller."

Stoller? Why did that name sound familiar? An unshaven face and the smell of cheap hair tonic came to mind. Yes, Clay remembered Stoller. He was an old client, an old job, back in '50 when the Whiz Kid Phillies won the National League pennant. The guy had opened a string of convenience stores after World War II just ahead of the 7-Eleven chain. Then he got involved in real estate in a big way, but still ran his business affairs out of a back office in his largest South

Philly store. After Clay got the call from Stoller, it was to that store he drove to get the lowdown on the assignment. For the sake of privacy they retired to the store's large walk-in refrigerator that backed glass cases of milk, beverages, and Oscar Mayer cold cuts. Yes, Clay saw it all vividly, probably a hell of a lot better than he had remembered it a week after it happened.

Stoller had Virginia hams for arms, stood maybe five-seven but weighed in as a middleweight. He winged an empty metal crate across the floor, then dragged a stack of milk bottles in place to begin dealing them onto the racks. "Where's your partner? I thought I'd be getting the main man."

"I told you he's out of town. On a job. Don't worry, we keep in touch." Clay leaned against the six-inch-thick insulated door. "So what's the trouble?"

"I'm being blackmailed."

"Any particular reason why?"

"Let's just say my business dealings. You don't need to know everything."

"I need to know more than that."

"You try to develop property in this town and you have to play the game. Now all of a sudden there's a special grand jury itching to make everything a crime."

"Which technically it is."

"It's business as usual. Philadelphia business as usual. Anybody could get nailed. You got to grease the wheels. The councilmen. The city inspectors. The cops. Everybody knows that."

"So everybody's threatening to drop your name to the grand jury?"

"The field's a little more narrow than that."

"How narrow?"

"My business partner is a top contender."

"Who's he and what's in it for him?"

"What do you think is in it for him? And maybe you heard of the guy. Montgomery Pembroke. A Main Line swell."

"On the subject of filthy rotten lucre, I get fifty bucks a day, plus expenses. Mind if I smoke?"

"We're in a Goddamn refrigerator!"

"Yeah, and I catch cold easy."

"Forty a day and a fin per diem. You seem a little young. If I'm getting the second string, I expect a discount."

"Thanks for your interest." Clay pushed his shoulder away from the door and turned to leave.

"Okay. Okay. Fifty bucks. The going rate."

"And two-fifty now as a retainer."Clay removed a small notebook and a pencil stub from the inside pocket of his jacket. "So feel free to unburden yourself and let me get started on earning that dough of yours. How'd you get mixed up with this Pembroke? Who is he?"

Stoller provided the abbreviated version, but over the years, Clay pieced together a fuller story. Pembroke wasn't the family name. It was Petrovsky. In the early 1800s, the patriarch of the family went from cabin boy to the owner of a fleet of clipper ships that traded in the Orient. His son became a shipping magnate in his own right, changed the family name to Pembroke, and made further fortunes in railroads and anthracite coal. Montgomery Senior, "Sonny," built the family estate in Lower Merion, the heart of the Main Line, and lived a life of leisure. Then came young Monty, Stoller's future business partner. During the 1920s, when he came of age, Pembroke wanted to make money faster than the clipping of coupons allowed. Like everybody else he played the stock market, using the bonds as collateral. When the stock market collapsed, he lost the bonds as the loans were called in. But Pembroke wasn't completely ruined because along the way he had begun investing in something unaffected by the crash.

"You have to give the guy credit," Stoller said. "He started running rum."

Pembroke moved Canadian rye, and while he didn't have enough time before the end of Prohibition to quite rebuild the family fortune, he was able to outfit a cruise ship in Florida and turn it into a floating casino that trolled just inside international waters. When German U boats made that too dangerous in 1942, Pembroke sold the ship as a troop transport at a sweetheart price. Pembroke and Stoller hooked up in Philly after World War II, their only common interest the accumulation of money.

"You don't sound like you come from here," Clay said.

"That's because I'm not."

The way Stoller told it, he showed up in the Quaker city as a penniless teenager. "I found work at a vegetable stand on the South Street market, saved my money, and opened my own stand."

During World War II, Stoller was drafted into the Army and became a supply sergeant. He continued to pad his bank account, mostly through craps and poker, but he was also willing to traffic in the black market whenever he came across some disposable goods.

"Everybody was doing it," he said. "Some of my best customers were majors and colonels."

Stoller returned from the war richer and shrewder. He opened his first convenience store and began dabbling in real estate. When the government made money available to clean up bad neighborhoods, Stoller began buying up property in Philadelphia and Chester, quicker than most to realize the profits that could be made from snapping up large stretches of rundown row houses.

"God damn, that was a field day," Stoller said. "And then I started having problems, thanks to Monty."

Pembroke had also learned about the potential of urban redevelopment. At some point he needed a parcel of land Stoller controlled, and when Stoller wouldn't accommodate him, Pembroke used his political connections to see that Stoller began to have permit problems.

"Still, I had to admire a guy with pull who knew how and was willing to use it."

Stoller didn't show any hard feelings when he finally gave up the property to Pembroke.

"Maybe I wasn't someone Pembroke would ever invite over for an afternoon of croquet and crumpets, but he could appreciate talent and suggested we go into business together. We started working the redevelopment angle together and have been feeding off the government tit ever since. I did the leg work and identified the properties while Pembroke made the phone calls to high places, hosted the lunches, and played the rounds of golf that cinched the deals. It was a mutually beneficial arrangement and we started to pile up the geld. At least I piled it up."

"Sounds like you and your partner have a beautiful relationship," Clay said. "So what makes you think the guy is blackmailing you?"

"Who else knows the dirt but him? Who else would hire a private dick to find out more? He sees what's happening with the grand jury. He knows it's going to be the little fish who are going to get fried, not the ones with the name and connections he has. I got no choice but to pay. And I sure as hell can't go to the cops."

"How do you make the payoff?"

"A key to a safety deposit box at a downtown bank was sent to me. I leave the money in the box, all tucked inside four different-sized envelopes. I number them smallest to largest. Somebody picks up the package. Nobody at the bank will tell me who's got the other key. Anyway, there's probably ten guys in between the blackmailer and the box."

"And how do you get the demands?"

"In the mail. Postmarked from all over the city."

"I want to see the letters."

"I don't need two people knowing my business. What I want you to do is dig up dirt on Pembroke. I need something to hold over him. Think you can handle the job?"

"What if there's no dirt on the guy?"

"I don't think that's going to be a problem."

"What if he's not the blackmailer?"

"Let me worry about that." Stoller blew on his hands and walked to the freezer door. "Just get me some dirt."

2

Vivian called from the kitchen, asking Clay how he wanted his coffee.

"Black as sin."

A hot cup of mud helped Clay to clear his head a little. He felt much better now. Just a little stiff. He rose from his chair and stretched his back. He looked out the window over the darkened sky of Philadelphia. In the distance he could see the lights of Boathouse Row shimmering in the Schuylkill River. It was a beautiful evening for a walk. Was there any reason to stay inside on such a night? He wasn't too old for a walk. It was quite a hike, but why not pay a visit to the boat houses? Hell, he already had his jacket on.

Clay walked to the door to leave, felt something in his waistband, looked down, and discovered a pistol. He paused before the front door, and pulled out the gun to look at it. Out of the corner of his eye something caught his attention. He turned to see a pair of legs protruding from a bathroom at the end of a brief hallway. Was somebody sick? Or was it something worse than that?

Cautiously, Clay approached the bathroom. He finally reached an angle where he could see a pool of blood that had spilled from some guy's head.

Clay looked at the gun. He looked at the body. "What happened?"

"Really? Again?"

Clay turned to see a young woman emerging from a kitchenette.

Vivian made him place the gun on the floor by the body, and soon he was sitting in an easy chair covered with sticky notes, sipping coffee, and writing a note to himself. "Focus." As he placed the note on one arm of the chair, he found two other notes with the same message. He picked up the pad and wrote another note. "You've been here before." He looked for a place to stick it on the other arm and noticed a previous message to himself. "It always seems like the first time."

Focus, he told himself. There was too much to take in all at once. Narrow it down. What about the girl? She was his granddaughter, but other than that, what did he remember? Smoke. He remembered blue smoke curling to the ceiling of some roadhouse. A girl just like this one was smoking a cigarette. That's right. The Stoller job. Clay wrote another note to himself. "Pembroke. Dirt."

With a society page picture of Pembroke provided by Stoller, Clay had driven to the Merion Golf Club in Ardmore where Pembroke was supposed to be entertaining a councilman. Clay parked down the road and waited for his mark to emerge through the club gates, then tailed him from a safe distance. Instead of heading into the city or returning home, Pembroke led

Clay to a roadhouse in Chester. Clay waited outside in the car for twenty minutes to make sure the guy wasn't just running an errand, and then entered the place, taking a stool at the bar to have a beer. Once his eyes adjusted to the dive's dim lighting, he searched for Pembroke in the long mirror that lined the back of the bar. Finally, Clay spotted his man in a booth sitting across from a pretty young blonde. She looked nothing like the *Inquirer* photo of the guy's auburn-haired wife. Looking a lot like Thomas E. Dewey, Pembroke was a pencil-thin-mustached rake with some well-placed gray at the temples. He squeezed the honey's hand on the tabletop and flashed the ivories as he chatted her up.

The front door opened. The sun illuminated the room for an instant, allowing Clay to see what a true dive this dive was. Cracked Naugahyde stools and benches. A wood floor that hadn't been refinished since Roosevelt. Teddy, not Franklin. Even the new Bubble Wurlitzer blaring dance tunes in the corner looked like it could use a polish. A guy wearing a Houndstooth-pattern hat and a red blazer was the newcomer. Once his eyes adjusted to the dark, the man located Pembroke and made his way over. Houndstooth removed a long envelope from the inside pocket of his blazer, pulled out a sheet of light blue paper, and handed it to Pembroke to read. A few seconds later he snatched back the paper, then turned and walked to the door. Pembroke peeled off the hand of the blonde trying to keep him from going, and hurried after the guy out the door and into the gravel parking lot.

For the next several minutes, Pembroke's date nursed

her drink, looking increasingly annoyed. She reached for a cigarette and opened a book of matches. Empty. She flipped the book aside looked around for the bartender, but he had gone to the back for something. She strolled to the bar, cigarette locked between her fingers, in search of a light, and maybe a fight to pick. By now it was obvious to Clay that her date was not coming back.

The only book of matches in sight lay next to Clay's beer. In the mirror he eyed her eyeing it, then laid his hand over the matches.

"You're new." The lady posed with the unlit cigarette at the end of a cocked arm.

"Can I buy you a drink?"

"That's original."

"Sorry. I'm new, remember?"

"Or maybe you've just been away for awhile. Maybe you're back from a stretch in prison. Or you got conked on the head and forgot who you were and wandered around the world for the past year. Maybe you could at least offer a lady a light."

Clay skipped the fold of matches across the bar in her direction. She looked at the matches, then took a longer look at Clay. She slipped past him to sit on the stool on the other side of him. "I think maybe I'll think about having that drink." As she took a seat, Clay noticed a fat diamond wedding ring crowding her fingers.

She slipped a nail between soft cherry lips. "Well?"

Clay retrieved the matches and struck a light for her, but held it in a way that forced her to lean down and draw closer to him. While she drew in the flame, she looked at him, then lifted her head and whistled a boiling cloud of pale blue smoke to the ceiling, the moment Clay would vividly recall many years later.

"So are you really new in town or just new to this watering hole?"

"What are you, the Welcome Wagon lady?"

"Could be I have a gift basket in the car with your name on it. Maybe you'd care for an ice scraper from the most honest mechanic around? The finest plumber in town sends his regards and a bottle opener. And I believe I might have a twelve-inch ruler courtesy of—but I'm sure you already have a twelve-inch ruler."

"Actually, I have a yardstick."

"Then you won't be needing the ruler."

"But sometimes you have a tight job and it comes in handy."

"And I'm sure you're a handy man."

"When I get the chance."

"Did you know the Welcome Wagon lady gets paid to bring you that little basket of promotional swag?"

"And I always thought she gave herself freely."

"Oh no! Not the Welcome Wagon lady. It's all business with the Welcome Wagon lady."

"She doesn't do it out of the goodness of her heart?"

"Don't be a sap. The Welcome Wagon lady always has an angle. And what about you, Yardstick? What's your angle? Why are you sitting in a bar in the middle of the day? Hawking insurance? The fish not biting?"

"Suppose the insurance game is beneath me. Suppose I'm working my way through college."

"A little old for the college racket. Maybe not, since the war. Besides, you're not the brainy type. I'd say you're pure action. Suppose you hit hard times."

"You should be a detective."

"Maybe it's the ponies that's got you. Or the booze. Or maybe even the junk."

"I'm sounding desperate."

"You live in a room with a hot plate."

"I don't cook."

"Who said you did?"

"Maybe I use the hot plate to cook my dope on a spoon."

"Exactly. And I bet you need money."

"Who doesn't?"

"You look tough enough to knock off a liquor store, but you're no common heist man. That's not the way you were raised."

"You've been talking to my father?"

"Over coffee. He said it was a waste of time to try to buy you off. With money, anyway. You're proud. You do things for your own reasons. He's a man who likes his coffee, your father."

"He's no Mormon."

"He also said you were a sucker for a damsel in distress."

"So I guess this is the part where I ask if you're in distress."

"No, this is the part where you say 'this is the part.'"

"So, are you in distress?"

"What girl isn't when she needs to be?" She stubbed out her cigarette and began to leave.

"What about that drink?"

"I'll take a rain check. I just wanted to welcome you to the neighborhood. Maybe we'll chat again sometime. See ya around . . . Yardstick."

Clay finished his beer and left. In the parking lot there was no sign of Pembroke's red Ferrari.

3

"Have you figured it out yet?" Sipping her coffee, Vivian looked down at Clay.

"The Welcome Wagon lady. So we meet again."

Vivian suggested Clay check the right-side pocket of his jacket.

After the reminder, Clay asked, "Where are we? What are we doing here?"

"We're waiting."

"For what?"

"A car to take us home. Just relax. It won't be long." Clay wondered why there were sticky notes all over the arm of the chair. He peeled one off and read, "The Three Musketeers." Who used to call him and his friends the Three Musketeers? Wasn't it the Reverend White, who used to laugh every time he repeated the line? Wait, was that his father? Everything was so muddled. He needed plenty of reminders. He was Clay White, right? He was the son of the Reverend and Mrs. Eben White, and he had two friends. Together, they became the Three Musketeers. Three became one. In the beginning there was Clay—the Preacher's Kid, the P.K.—the child who had all the advantages but somehow strayed off the path no matter how his parents tried. He was Clay White. He had to hold onto that fact. He was sitting in a chair he didn't know where, waiting for a car to take him somewhere else for no apparent reason. He had to hold onto something. He was Clay White, the preacher's kid. He was always getting into trouble and sent to his father's study to await the return of The Rev. That's what the Three Musketeers called his father, right? "The Rev."

What was that story, the first time Clay really pissed off his mother? She was always wound a little tight. It wasn't easy being the perfect Mrs. Reverend Eben White. The flock could gossip and indulge their vanities, but not her. She had to sit in the first row of pews, hands shackled in stiff sugar-white gloves, and actually pay attention to The Rev when he delivered his message. She had no shortage of crosses to bear, either. For one thing, she was taller than The Rev. Talk about shame! She stood five-nine, while he was a five-four bantam rooster. Worse than that, she was older by two years. But the heaviest cross of all was her nicked lip. She had been born with a cleft lip and palette, left uncorrected until several years after her birth, more than enough time for her to grow deeply ashamed of her appearance. The Rev had explained it all to Clay one day when he thought Clay was old enough to understand. After the procedure, all that remained was a notch in her upper lip that was hardly noticeable. Still, she was always coughing or yawning, covering her mouth, looking bored when she spoke to people.

The ladies of the church didn't appreciate her acting so superior just because she was the wife of the minister. Mrs. White didn't help anything by turning down all of the dinner invitations she and The Rev received.

When he was maybe six years old, Clay lost his mother. He was drawing crayon pictures with his younger cousin Ruth on the living room floor of the rectory. He had looked over to see what his cousin was drawing. It was some kind of frenzied thing in black and green. Clay then made the mistake of asking Ruth what she had in mind.

"It's your mommy," she said. "Can't you see?"

"But that's so . . . ugly."

"Didn't you know? Your mommy's ugly."

Ruth held up her portrait. Taking a closer look, Clay began to find order in what at first glance appeared to be mere chaos. A hideous face took shape. A hooked nose. Dark, cavernous nostrils. A chin with a mole on it. A wrinkled neck. And a lip with a deep red gash.

Clay ripped the picture from his cousin's hands. She screamed and began to wrestle him for the paper.

Clay pulled the drawing away from his cousin just as his mother, wearing only a cotton slip, rushed in to investigate. Her hair was down, the tresses snaking over her shoulders and curling around her fallen breasts. Clay released his cousin, who sat on the floor wailing. Clay looked at his mother, he looked at the picture, comparing the two with open-mouth horror.

"See what he drew!" his cousin said.

Clay's mother looked at the picture. Her mouth with its scarred lip dropped open. She quickly covered it with her hand.

"That's her picture!" Clay cried.

"Lying only make things worse!" Clay's mother sent him to his father's study to await the return of The Rev and the meting out of appropriate punishment.

The Rev's study, that was another part of the story of how things began going horribly wrong between Clay and his parents. The study was the Rev's garage, a place where he kept his tools and liked to tinker on a soul in his spare time. When the door was open, the two other musketeers could not resist pausing on the way to Clay's bedroom to gaze upon what seemed like a place of awe and wonder to them. Instead of a girlie calendar on the wall like they glimpsed inside the garage at the local service station, there was a promotional calendar courtesy of the Landis Funeral Home, "Where your sorrow is our business." Across from the desk was the Rev's work space, an oversized chair. The sinner's chair. Both of Clay's friends tried it out. The sinner's chair was not made for comfort. Far from it. Not only were cushions nonexistent, the slick fake leather fastened itself to bare skin that would then have to be peeled free before the sinner was set free. There were also thick buttons, half-dollar in size, that were perfectly placed on the arms and back of the chair to produce maximum discomfort.

Over the years, Clay spent untold hours sitting in the sinner's chair waiting for his father to return home, staring at the latest funeral home calendar. Spring pictures gave way to summer scenes, followed by depictions of the fall and winter, and then a fresh calendar was tacked to the wall and the cycle began anew. But the slogan never changed. Sorrow, apparently, never went out of fashion. Clay sat in that chair, year after year, and those half-dollar buttons never failed to irritate no matter how tall he grew.

One afternoon, when Clay was about nine years old, his father said nothing as he entered his study and sat at his desk. He clasped his hands, closed his eyes, and mouthed a brief, silent prayer. With his head still bowed, The Rev cracked his eyelids and peered up at Clay, brown pupils rimming the crest of his red-splintered eyes. "I have reached my limit, young man."

"I'm sorry, Father."

"'Sorry' is far from good enough at this juncture. I think you need friends. Do you have any friends, Clay?"

"I don't know."

"If you don't know, then you don't have any."

Friends? Did the Reverend and Mrs. White have any friends? The Rev spent a lot of time with Mr. Landis at the funeral home delivering eulogies, true. But they weren't friends; they were more like business associates. Your sorrow was their joint venture. And did his mother have any friends? The ladies in church were little more than annoying constituents. Clay could not think of any friends his parents had, aside from the Reverend Bones and his wife who paid an occasional visit from Maryland, where he had a church. Father and Reverend Bones had attended seminary together. Oh, the stories they could tell! Only they never did.

"Clay, have you noticed that a new family has moved in down the block and now attends the church? They have a boy your age. Charles."

"Chuck. He's in my class."

"Well, this Chuck could probably use a friend. I want you to be his friend."

"What if I don't like him?"

"You don't have to like someone to be their friend, Clay. Sometimes it's better that you don't like them. It can cloud your judgment."

"I'll try."

"I'm not asking you to try."

"I will."

"That's the spirit. Now go." With the usual wave of the Rev's hand, Clay was dismissed. Go forth and multiply your friends.

And that was the genesis of the Three Musketeers.

4

Clay returned the sticky note with "the Three Musketeers" to its place on the chair. He was still not sure what he was trying to remember, but he was certain he was trying to remember something important. All these sticky notes clinging to the Lazy Boy in no particular order, he needed to arrange them. He needed a system. Clay peeled off all of the notes on the right arm of the chair, and transferred them to the left arm and within reach down the left side of the chair. With the right arm now empty, he pasted the Three Musketeers' note at arm's length, the top of a new list.

"I'll give you one thing, grandpa, you're persistent."

Clay looked up to see a young woman, legs crossed, sitting at a small dinette table. At her suggestion, he removed a pair of notes in his jacket pocket and placed him on the right arm of the Lazy Boy. At the head of the list he now placed "She's your granddaughter. Vivian." Below that went "Barrett." After conferring further with his supposed granddaughter, Clay wrote a replacement note. "Barrett: murder victim." Below that note, Clay relocated "the Three Musketeers." Clay studied his arrangement, trying to keep in mind what he understood so far.

Clay turned his attention to "Barrett: murder victim." That was the whole point, wasn't it? This was a murder investigation, right? Clay asked the girl who this Barrett guy was.

"Steve's brother. Step-brother actually," she said.

"Steve?"

"My husband Steve."

Clay wrote a fresh note with "Steve" written on it, and added it to his column of yellow Post-Its. Did he remember a Steve? Clay closed his eyes and a cigar came to mind. Attached to the cigar were lips, lips that declared, "Hundred bucks a hole? Hell, I bet you don't have a hundred bucks to your name."

Steve and some other kid were loosening up at the first tee at a country club golf course, gripping fat drivers overhead and twisting side to side. Clay sat in an electric cart, not playing, just out for the sun and the camaraderie of the young people. At the moment, they were haggling over the bet for the morning's round.

"What do you think, Clay? Is your boy good for it when I wax his ass?"

"My boy?"

"Sure. Tom's your boy. Didn't you know, you're his role model, you and that hardboiled life you led back in the day."

"You taking the bet or not?" This Tom fellow was ready to go, pressing a ball and tee between his thumb and first two fingers like a hypodermic needle.

Pembroke was the kid's name. Tom Pembroke. Clay knew his dad and his grandfather before that.

They finally settled on a hundred a hole, but for all his talk young Pembroke did not play well. He kept losing holes and on the eighteenth doubled the bet in hopes of drawing even. But on a five-footer that would have won the hole, he yanked the putt. They halved the hole, and Tom lost his chance to salvage the morning.

A fresh cigar wagged in Steve's mouth as he spoke. "Usually I'd accept a check, only I'm not so sure in your case."

"Fuck you very much."

Steve clapped Clay on the shoulder. "Tommy boy is like his golf game. All show and no dough."

Tom raised his putter and chased Steve off the green, looking like he was angry enough to bash in his skull. They were both laughing, horsing around like old buddies, but it wasn't clear that if given the chance Tom might not put that putter to better effect than he had on the eighteenth. After Steve managed to place a sand trap between them, Tom marched back to his cart, unzipped a pocket of his bag, and pulled out a pistol.

Stiff-armed, Tom raised the gun to eye level. "What were you saying, Motherfucker?"

"Are you crazy? Put that thing away."

"You were saying something?"

"Somebody's going to see you."

"You think I'm funny?"

"Why do you carry that thing around? What is with you, Tom, and this tough guy act?"

"You think this is an act?"

"You're going to get us in trouble. Put it away."

31

"After you dance for me."

"Oh, shit!" Steve yelped. No more smiles and nervous laughter. "I think a bee stung me."

"You poor thing." Tom palmed the gun against his leg and glanced around to see if anyone was looking.

"My kit's back home in the other car. Jesus fucking Christ. Somebody call 911."

"Take it easy. You have plenty of time." Tom walked back to the cart to stash the pistol.

Apparently Steve didn't have plenty of time. Clay remembered the guy's funeral. Clay's granddaughter was there, black veiled and sobbing, tucked under his arm. They stood under a tent and looked down at a casket suspended by straps. The thing was, Steve did not die from an allergic reaction to the bee sting. The ambulance crew was to blame. Instead of hooking up an IV drip with something to calm him down, the para-fuckups grabbed the wrong bag and shot the kid full of lidocaine. The anesthetic threw him into a fit and flatlined his heart for half a minute before Laurel and Hardy could untangle the paddles to the defibrillator and slap them to his chest. By the time they got him to the hospital, the damage had been done. Steve managed to hang on for a few days but it was only a matter of time before his body caught up with his scrambled brain.

As Clay and his granddaughter walked together from the burial plot to the funeral home limo, Pembroke slipped between them to take her hand. Squeezing it, he said, "It's going to be all right. Remember, I'm here for you."

"That means a lot to me."

At the dinner afterwards, she had no time for Pembroke, who occasionally tried to stand or sit next to Vivian. She always found reason to move away. Eventually Pembroke sat next to Clay, patting him on the knee. "How you doing, sir?"

"Huh?"

"Not feeling too lucid today, I guess."

"Huh?"

"Right on." Pembroke glanced around the room. "Nice turnout for Steve. Did you read the obit in the *Inquirer?*"

"Huh?"

"They made it seem like Steve was the most righteous guy in the world." Pembroke looked in the direction of Vivian, who was laughing with a pair of older ladies. "And they were just the perfect young couple. Big tippers at the club. All the waiters and doormen adored them. On the board of this and that charity. Real down to earth. Yeah, well, he's real down to earth now. God, I could use a bowl. What about you, Mr. White? Wanna get high?"

"Huh?"

"The good thing about you, Clay, is you don't remember shit. The water just keeps passing under the bridge."

"I can remember if I want to. I just don't want to."

"Well, the doctors did say there's no major loss of brain cells. Maybe you're just scamming us."

"Huh?"

"Then again, maybe not."

An old family friend, Phyllis Ryan, crossed the room to greet Clay then turned to Pembroke. "You seem to be holding up all right."

"I don't look devastated enough for you?"

"You are such a wicked boy."

"Be honest, Phyllis, how much money you really think Vivian's looking at once everything gets settled? Besides her share of the company, I mean."

"There will be time enough for all that."

"Come on. I thought I could always count on you to be blunt."

"Blunt. Not crass. You know I've always liked you, Tom, but you need to learn to keep at least some of your thoughts to yourself and to bide your time. And show some Goddamn respect for the departed, dearly or not."

"Bide my time? Until I'm like Clay here?"

"I'm older than Clay, and I'm still here."

"Still biding your time?"

Phyllis smiled and walked away.

A minute later Vivian paid a visit. She kissed Clay on the temple. "Thanks for keeping him company, Tom."

"I've always liked your grandfather, you know that."

"I think he's getting tired."

"I'm not tired," Clay said.

"Would you mind taking him home?"

Pembroke drove Clay to his house where a care provider waited. Pembroke cupped a pipe while he drove. "She's trying to get rid of me with a smile. The bitch is trying to get rid of me. I guess all that talk was just talk. She doesn't need me now. The fucking bitch. She doesn't think she needs me now. Well man, she's fucking wrong. This deal's not over. Not by half."

"Huh?"

5

Clay reviewed his list of notes on the chair. He felt he was beginning to get somewhere. Just as his memories were starting to gel, he was struck by the image of a body being dragged through the leaves, followed quickly by the sight of someone in a dark room begging for his life, and the image of an old man wearing a ushanka, its furry earflaps popping in the air after a blow to the jaw. Those memories were quickly overwhelmed by a blizzard of other memories. Disjointed, unconnected memories, none that could be singled out. It was just a swirl, a maddening collective howl. Clay closed his eyes and bore it the best he could until it passed. And on the other side, he started fresh. Regrets? He had a few, but then again, too few to mention.

"Grandpa." A voice cut through the noise. "Are you okay?"

Clay opened his eyes and focused on a girl's face. She seemed concerned. "Do I know you?" he asked.

Vivian referred him to the notes on his chair. Apparently someone had been killed, some kid named

Barrett, and Clay had been hired by a guy named Stoller to find out who did the deed. There were three primary suspects, including Steve, who he assumed was one of the Three Musketeers. But wasn't Steve dead? You had to rule him out. Obviously, Clay needed a little more guidance on the case.

"Where's Stoller?" Clay asked.

"Who?" Vivian said.

"The client."

"You don't have a client, grandpa. That was probably from years ago."

That's right, it was a job from a long time ago. But it felt connected somehow. It was his only solid lead and he had to follow it. He remembered tailing Stoller's business partner, some guy named Pembroke, and meeting a girl at the roadhouse. The next day, armed with a cardboard cup of coffee, a couple of sinkers in a bag, and the morning paper, Clay kept watch on the entrance to Pembroke's estate. After all these years had passed, he retained a vivid image of the newspaper as if it were still in his hands. He could feel the newsprint, the fingers on his one hand smudged and greasy from ink, the fingers of the other warm from the coffee container and gritty with doughnut crumbs.

Clay scanned the headlines. MacArthur was driving the North Koreans out of the South, and maybe just as important, a Philadelphian, Marine Sergeant Robert J. Bowden, made the first flying saucer sighting of the war. The Crime Committee headed by Tennessee Senator Estes Kefauver had also brought their traveling circus to town. Months earlier, a Kansas City gambler had been found dead in a Democratic Party clubhouse, right below a picture of Harry Truman. An obvious gangland hit. After the war, organized crime had gotten a bit too disorganized for everybody's liking, and so the Senate had set up a special committee under Kefauver to investigate organized crime in interstate commerce. The Senators were holding hearings across the country on their way to New York and a televised round. Like always, Philly was just part of the out-of-town circuit where most shows bound for Broadway worked out the kinks.

Further down the front page, Clay read the latest on the big spy case, the ring that gave the Soviets the dope on how to make the atom bomb. It was looking like this Julius Rosenberg character had recruited some Army sergeant at the Los Alamos laboratory, his brother-in-law, to obtain the information. Rosenberg tore a Jello box top in half and gave one end to the sergeant and the other to a courier who showed up one day with the other half.

Box top. Clay began peeling off notes from the left side of the Lazy Boy and inspecting them. "Harris." "Snake Alley." "Miles Archer." "9DP36." Finally, he found it. "Box top." Clay placed the note on the right arm of the chair.

Clay returned his thoughts to the newspaper he had read years ago. Buried deep within the pages, he had come across a short notice about a murder victim found in a wooded area in Montgomery County. A young man, no identification, broken neck, covered in leaves. Clay skipped to the sports section to catch up on the Phillies. His coffee was still warm, one doughnut untouched, and the game account of the Phillies' loss half-read when the sound of a blaring horn caused him to look up. And there she was again, the blonde from the roadhouse, wearing a little black dress, standing behind the open door of a matching black roadster and palming the horn for five seconds at a belt. A negro at the gate tried to quiet her, but no luck. A minute later, Pembroke came to the gate looking as peeved as a cool customer deigned to look and tried to chase her away with a smile. Clay couldn't hear the conversation, but it was obvious she wasn't going anywhere soon. Only after she had her say was Pembroke able to nod and nudge and humor her back into her car. He gave her a token wave as she finally drove off. As soon as she was out of sight, he snapped at the negro manning the gate.

Clay turned over the engine, pulled away from the curb, and caught up to the roadster. Juggling his coffee while shifting gears, he lagged behind at a comfortable distance and followed the girl. She stopped to pick up another woman, an older peroxide blonde, and drove to Wanamaker's department store. Rather than grow bored in his parked sedan, Clay decided to shadow them inside. He watched the ladies try on hats and gloves and shoes for two hours and arrange to have their packages sent home. He then tailed them to a restaurant where they had lunch, followed by more shopping before the one called it quits and Pembroke's girl decided to go to the movies. She picked a double feature. While she watched the movies by herself, nursing a small box of popcorn, Clay sat in the back and watched her watch the screen.

As the second show came to an end, Clay slipped out of the theater and set up shop across the street behind a newspaper and a cigarette. When she appeared, some wolf who must have spotted her in the movie house was hot on the trail. He skipped in front of her and walked backwards to throw in his line. She didn't bite, she didn't even acknowledge that he spoke. But the guy didn't give up so easily. Maybe he was a soft-soap man, used to working on commission, and knew the secret to sales was to just keep pitching. He touched her elbow. She batted his hand away and continued walking. He grabbed her elbow. That was going too far, and she winged a right at him. It came too wide, giving him plenty of time to get up his guard and snatch her wrist.

Clay tossed the paper in a can and crossed the street as the girl and the go-getter began to tussle. In the meantime, a half-dozen good citizens passed by, not one of them about to interfere in what they probably convinced themselves was just a lover's quarrel.

"That's enough." Clay flicked his cigarette in the gutter.

"That is a private concern. Keep moving, Bub."

"Will you call the cops?" she said. "I don't know this masher."

"Aw, that's what you always say. Now cut the crap, honey. We're going home. It ain't much but it's all ours. There's our ride two cars up."

"I told you nice to let her go," Clay said.

"And I thought I told you nice to shove off."

"Is that you, Yardstick?" She smiled at Clay.

"Yeah, it's me. Ain't this funny. Looks like you developed a tumor the size of a jerk."

"You two know each other?" The guy was already easing up on his grip.

"You feel like getting to know me, too?"

"I know how to handle myself, Bub. I was in the Navy."

"In the galley scrambling eggs, maybe. Do you want to compare discharge papers or do you want to mix?"

The guy gave it a half-second's worth of thought, then dropped her arm. "I got better things to do." He walked away slow and tough, but he walked away just the same.

Two hours later Clay knew the name of Pembroke's girl. Her first name, at least. Lynne. He was in the passenger's seat of her roadster parked past midnight, the motor idling, in a narrow Philadelphia alley. His own dented Dodge was parked behind them. They were supposed to be sampling some hot jazz from St. Louis skipping cross-country over the night air on KMOX radio. Instead, he was being treated to an extended complaint, a riff on why her husband was a mean old skin-flint for dumping this used car on her. "Maybe it only had 5,000 miles when he bought it, that is if you could trust the odometer, but it didn't have the showroom smell, and that ruined the entire experience."

"Once you drive it a block, every car becomes a used one," Clay said

"That's not the point. My husband is a cheapskate. He could have bought me a new one, but he didn't because he wanted to save a few bucks. I swear to God, darling, if something were ever to happen to him I wouldn't be sorry."

"'Darling,' is it?"

"I'm just saying it's not fair." The girl knew how to pout. The limp lower lip. Just enough tears to glisten the eyes. A slight catch in her throat. "Sometimes I wish a big black rock fell off the side of a mountain and landed on the roof of his car."

"I guess that would make you a widow. A rich, young, desirable widow."

"Who doesn't look good in black?"

"You're wearing black right now."

"Maybe I'm getting in some practice."

"All that's missing is the veil and lace hanky."

"I never cared much for veils," she said. "Would it be too scandalous if I didn't wear one?"

"That depends."

"On what?"

"The jury."

"You think too much, Yardstick. Are you ever going to kiss me?"

"We hardly know each other."

"That's such a bad thing? Maybe the less you know somebody the less chance they'll have to disappoint you."

"And you're a married woman. For the time being, at least."

"Your point is?" She pulled him by the lapel and as their lips met, the jazz from KMOX swelled as a cloud uncovered the moon. She retreated a couple of inches. "How would you like to start your own business?"

"Maybe I already got my own business."

"I mean the kind with a cash register. Stuffed all nice and green. The kind with a shiny bell over the door that

41

rings every time a sucker walks in. Ting-a-ling-a-ling."
She began to unbuckle his belt, then stopped. "You're
using me."

"Not if you get there first."

She pushed Clay aside and began straightening her
hair. "Ever since I turned fifteen I've had to deal with
your type. All talk, talk, talk, but you never keep your
promises."

"What, to drop a rock on poppy?"

"Accidents happen."

"No, they don't."

"Funny how you suddenly showed up tonight in my
moment of need."

"Luck."

"You make your own luck. I think you were following
me. Take it from a girl who's been followed before."

"And what if I grant you that point?"

"Get out of my car."

A second later, Clay was slamming the door and
walking to his Dodge.

Lynne cranked open her window. "You don't have to
get so touchy. Come back."

Clay ignored her, turned over the engine of his
Dodge, and drove off.

6

Barrett: murder victim. The suspects: the Three Musketeers. Wait. Weren't they just kids? And hadn't he been one of the Three Musketeers? In the beginning was Clay, without form and void. The Rev then insisted that Clay make friends with the new kid in school, Chuck Lefebvre. Chuck's parents had been just as eager as The Rev to have the boys become friends. Chuck's father was a smooth-talking insurance salesman, his mother a former harvest queen. Like Clay, Chuck had a certain image to live up to. And failed. When people saw Chuck they were supposed to see his old man, gain trust in him, and by implication the policies sold by the Town and Country Fire and Life Insurance Co. Instead, Chuck was chubby and suffered from a wandering eye. He struggled in school, had a penchant for making inappropriate comments, and even at a young age was smut-obsessed. Was it for this that Mr. Lefebvre worked so hard and misled so many? The family attended church every Sunday morning. Mr. Lefebvre glad-handed half the congregation with a two-fisted grip that oozed confidence and made you check to see if your wristwatch was still in place when he moved on to the next pew. Chuck's honey-haired mother worked the room in her own fashion, drawing the admiration of the men and the ire of the women of the church. And then there was Chuck. He spoke to none of the children in the basement Sunday School and barely whispered when called upon by the teachers. In public school he said even less.

"Who would have ever thought he was quiet?" Clay said.

"Who, Grandpa?"

"Chuck. My friend Chuck. Don't you remember him?"

"Are you sure you remember him?"

That was a good question. Didn't he remember that at the lunch table at school Chuck invited Clay over to his house. That happened, right? He spent an entire afternoon in Chuck's bedroom, mostly listening to Chuck. His silence, it turned out, had been vastly overrated. Chuck jabbered on about how he was going to grow up some day to become a soldier or a sheriff just so he could kill people and not get in trouble for it.

"Want to see some real merchandise," Chuck said. He pulled a broken kite that hid a soap box filled with colorful stock certificates that he said his father had given him. They were securities from obscure companies that his father peddled on the side.

"This is my favorite." Chuck held the face of the certificate to his chest. "The Ponzi Motor Company." He slowly turned it around to show a buxom woman wielding a sword in one hand and clutching a hubcap as a shield in the other, hair blowing in the wind, gossamer gown clinging to her breasts and thighs. "She's got plenty of snap in her garter, am I right?"

"I guess so."

"Maybe Ponzi doesn't have an actual office, and nobody's seen one of their cars on the road, but so what? Anyone can build a stupid car. But not everybody can sell stock! Now's the time to get in on it! Nineteen-twenty-nine isn't going to last forever, you know."

Of course, a couple weeks later, the stock market crashed. At least Chuck could now have all the lurid stock certificates a boy could ever want.

So, that was the second musketeer. But what about the third? Clay stared at the sticky note with "the Three Musketeers" written on it. The three of them were inseparable. There was Clay, then Chuck, then... Johnny. Yes, of course, there was Johnny. Clay, Chuck, and Johnny. He didn't have a clear picture in his head of Johnny, but he knew he was one of the Three Musketeers. Johnny had come to the country from the crowded streets of Philadelphia's Southwark district. He had told the whole story to Clay and Chuck, but that was only after they became friends. Johnny told them how his dad had worked the docks as a stevedore. The family didn't have much, just an apartment and some Sears and Roebuck furniture bought on time. Plenty of Southwark men, maybe most of them, drank their pay envelops at the bars and cellar gin shops in the neighborhood, but not John LeMaster. It wasn't like he lacked for trouble, most of which he blamed on the dock foreman always riding him and making his days miserable. Johnny's dad was always a little

45

grumpy. Mom said it was his own damn fault. He was always the Gloomy Gus, never happy with anything. She should talk, of course. Not one day passed that she didn't wish she had never left the farm to find work and excitement and, yes, a husband in Philadelphia. Well, now she had her city man, a hardworking breadwinner, but did that make her happy?

"She said she could only be happy if he was happy, but he wasn't happy, so she couldn't be happy," Johnny said. "Besides, she wasn't feeling too good after awhile."

When Johnny's mom took ill, his dad didn't believe it was anything serious. Soon it became obvious that this wasn't just one of her moods. They avoided the expense of a doctor for as long as they could, that was the Southwark way, and when they finally called in one, it was too late. Like sweet Molly Malone they sang about in school, she died of a fever and no one could save her and she was buried the Southwark way. No ceremony. Scant mourning. She was just gone, bagged up and tipped through the bottom of a booby-hatch coffin the undertaker kept for such purposes, dumped into a common grave. Southwark the whole way.

"I pretended she had just gone around the corner to the bakery and would be back any minute. I swear to god, I believed that for two weeks."

"Seriously?" Chuck had said. "I wish I could make my brain work like that. I'd have me a good time!"

Of course, Johnny's mother never came back. His father didn't handle her loss well, either. He finally lost his patience with the foreman one day, and they got into a brawl on the pier. A real give and take. Nobody had ever managed to best the foreman, but John

LeMaster came through and might have even finished off the guy if the other men hadn't pulled him off. As it was, LeMaster lost his job, and all the other pier owners blackballed him, even though they knew he had just lost his wife. Out of work with a young boy on his hands, LeMaster had few options. Look for a job in another line of endeavor and probably be belittled by some new foreman, was that his hope for the future?

"One day, my Dad told me to pack a cardboard grip he just bought from Woolworths. Then we took the trolley to the Broad Street Station and hopped a train."

Not knowing where they were headed, Johnny watched the station signs slide past the window: Paoli, Downingtown, Parkesburg. Finally when the train pulled into Lancaster, his father told him to fetch his grip. An hour later, they caught a bus that took them to Johnny's grandfather, who had never liked Johnny's dad and wasn't happy that his daughter was put in the ground before he had even heard she was ailing. He was even more upset when he learned that LeMaster was leaving Johnny with him while he attended to business.

Those were tough times for everyone, the years after the stock market crash. Although the Reverend White owned no stock, his income dwindled because of the crash. There was certainly no shortage of customers for his trade, the pews filled by people who were deep in debt, who had lost their jobs or were about to lose the family farm, but they were not inclined to pony up when the collection plate made the rounds on a Sunday morning. The weekly haul steadily decreased, forcing a cut in the pastor's salary. Considering how poorly his flock was faring, The Rev did not complain about his drop in pay. That did not prevent him from grumbling about the root of the country's problems, both from the pulpit and at the dinner table. He placed the blame squarely where it belonged: the Communist Party. The Reds were obviously behind the stock market crash.

Clay and Chuck were best friends by the time they met Johnny, not because Clay liked Chuck, he didn't, but because it was ordained that they should be best friends. Unfortunately, the Reverend and Mrs. White did not see any noticeable change in Clay's behavior after he befriended the neighbor boy. Maybe he required a group of friends. He certainly needed to learn how to work well with others and develop leadership skills. When his parents heard that there was yet another new boy in Clay's class, Johnny, they urged him to seek out and befriend the new boy and to encourage Chuck to do so as well. That was how Johnny was to become one of the Three Musketeers.

Clay and Chuck had decided to make friends with Johnny at recess one morning. So far, he hadn't shown much in class, never having an answer to offer when called upon. He was just a sullen boy wearing patched overalls.

Johnny stood on the edge of the playground watching some of the other boys playing baseball when Clay and Chuck approached. Clay took the lead, as was expected of the son of a minister. "Welcome to town."

"We're just saying this because we have to," Chuck said.

"Cripes, Chuck!"

"Sorry."

"We're trying to be friendly."

"Okay. Fine. I'll make conversation. So, Johnny, what's your dad do?"

"My dad?" Johnny cocked an eye.

"I mean, what kind of work is he looking for?"

"You want to know about my dad?"

"Yeah, what's he do?"

Johnny glanced down and toed the ground like a pitcher on the rubber. Finally he looked up and said, "My dad's a Communist."

7

Clay tried to remember when he had started to forget. How had his mind come to this? He was sitting in a hotel easy chair, trying to solve a murder that had apparently just taken place, but it may as well have happened a hundred years ago. Barrett: murder victim. He had to constantly remind himself by looking at the sticky note that a murder had taken place. Stoller had hired him to find out who killed this Barrett character. But wasn't Stoller being blackmailed? And what about the box top? Clay was having trouble holding onto anything.

So, just when did his memory get so bad? Actually, it wasn't a question of forgetting things. Once started, he couldn't stop the flow of memories. That was the real problem. And they weren't just any memories. They weren't the good times that came flooding back. It was the disappointments. The shameful moments. The regrets that pile up in life.

Clay blamed baseball. It all started with Chico Ruiz stealing home. It was all Chico's fault. Clay couldn't stop remembering the bad moments, and Chico Ruiz stealing home was one of the worst. Clay was at that game against Cincinnati in September 1964. The Phillies had just split a four-game series with the Dodgers and were in first place by six-and-a-half games with little more than two weeks left in the season. The World Series was all but a certainty. Then, Cuban rookie infielder Chico Ruiz stole home and nothing would ever be the same. For Philadelphia or for Clay. From where he sat in a box seat on the first base side, Clay had a clear view of the play. Ruiz's twitching leg caught his attention. Clay realized that the kid was about to break for home. He's got Frank Robinson at the plate and he's thinking about stealing home? It made no sense, yet a moment later Ruiz darted for the plate and slid in safely.

Ruiz's reckless play was little more than a curiosity at the moment. The Phillies had four innings to match the run, but they couldn't and lost the game, 1-0. Nine straight losses followed as the Phillies blew the pennant. The entire city was stunned by the collapse, and in time were more scarred than stunned. It was one of those moments in life that Clay would rather forget. But he couldn't.

"It's just a game," Clay's wife said when it was all over on the final Sunday afternoon in October 1964.

That was when he hit her for the first time. It wouldn't be the last. Another memory he wished he could erase.

Why should Clay recall so much about Chico Ruiz? The guy played eight seasons in the major leagues, never did much, other than get in trouble for pulling a gun on a teammate in a clubhouse fight. He never actually retired from the game. His career ended when he wrapped his car around a sign pole early one morning. He was not mourned in Philadelphia, nor was he forgotten. Over the years, his steal of home, his stupid rookie dash for glory, was seen as the nail that lost the shoe that lost the '64 pennant.

It was sometime in the 1980s that Clay began to dream of that moment he had sat in the stands and watched Chico Ruiz edging off of third base. Soon, that image of the rookie's twitching leg began to appear to Clay during his waking hours. It was a recurring image that he just couldn't shake.

Rather than television, Clay preferred listening to the Phillies' games on the radio sitting on the verandah of his Main Line home. He made it to Veteran's Stadium a few times each summer as well, but as the losses mounted in the '80s, Clay found himself studying the sports pages less and devoting more attention to the news. He was fascinated by the exploits of Philly mobster Nicky Scarfo. Little Nicky, who by way of Atlantic City ascended the ranks of the Philadelphia underworld in bloody fashion to become the face of Philly crime.

Mostly, Clay followed the international news, especially the developments in Eastern Europe and the Soviet Union. It was also during this time that his memory problems began to worsen. Just as the Soviets allowed more freedom of speech, Clay's hold on his memories began to slip. He often found his mind racing and had difficulty concentrating for more than a few seconds at a time. He was overwhelmed by moments in his life that he would prefer to keep buried. It seemed that the more the Poles and Germans, the Czechs and Slovaks exerted their freedom, the more Clay had to face a lifetime of regret.

And then the Wall came down.

Clay's problem only escalated as the Soviet Union unraveled. Clay could barely follow the events on television, Boris Yeltsin standing on a tank to ward off the coup attempt of hardliners and all the rest of it. Then 9/11 came and the situation grew even worse. Clay was assailed by a lifetime of regrets. The images crowded into one another. Someone pleaded for his life. Someone else dared him to do it. A body covered in leaves. Chico Ruiz making a dash for home. Individually the memories were too much to shoulder. Allowed to run together, stirred up into a mass of images, however, they were robbed of their individual sting. Pure confusion was a better option, and so Clay nurtured the confusion. He retreated into the confusion as necessary, but gradually the attacks of regret grew relentless, forcing him to take shelter from the storm more often. Rare became the moments of lucidity in his life. He was lucky to make his way to the kitchen before forgetting his purpose. He was unable to hold onto any thought for very long. He was so haunted by the past, he lost his grip on the present.

It was his granddaughter who finally persuaded Clay to see someone about his memory problem. To please Vivian—as if he had a choice—he paid a visit to a neurologist. Clay took a battery of tests and underwent a CT scan. The neurologist concluded that while there was no evidence of deterioration to the brain, Clay was clearly suffering from an advanced form of dementia. The verdict angered Clay, enough to overshadow the regrets for a while.

"I'm not crazy." Clay didn't care for the neurologist or the pictures of his family on his desk. If he had such a great memory, why did he need pictures?

"This is not a matter of sanity, Mr. White. Merely a question of cognition."

"It's not my memory you should be worried about, it's my heart attacks!"

"Grandpa, he's just trying to help." Vivian gripped the back of Clay's hand. She was sitting with him along with Steve, who had reluctantly agreed to delay a golf date to show some familial support. He was dressed for the course and the fingers of his gloves spilled out of a back pocket.

"Your heart is fine, Mr. White. Your lungs are fine."

"Are you wearing a wire?"

"I beg your pardon?"

"Are you wearing a wire?"

"Did you tell him about the letters?" Steve asked Vivian.

"No."

"He's constantly reading these old letters."

"That's not so unusual," the neurologist said. "It's a generational thing. A lot of my older patients like to read letters they've kept over the years."

"They're old, but they aren't letters he received. They're letters he never sent. Stacks of them."

"Mr. White," the neurologist said. "Why did you never send the letters?"

"What letters?

"The letters you're always reading, why did you never send them?"

"I must not have had a stamp."

"Why do you read the letters, Mr. White?"

"To remind me who I am."

"That's good, right?" Vivian said. "He's trying to stay aware."

"Fine. Encourage him to read as much as he wants. In fact..." The neurologist reached for a prescription pad. "I'm going to write him something that might help a little."

"Doctor, have you heard of a place called Shady Arms?" Steve asked. "A friend's grandfather just moved in. He seems to like it."

"Excellent facility."

"Is that what you recommend, an institution?" Vivian asked.

"Perhaps later. I think he'll be happier at home for the time being. Familiar surroundings. His letters. Let's try the medication first."

"I'm sitting right here. Am I invisible?" Clay said.

"Make sure he has something in his stomach twenty minutes before." The neurologist handed Vivian a slip of paper. "The directions will be on the prescription."

"Hello!" Clay waved a hand.

"Thank you, Doctor."

"I suppose you're wondering why I called you all here today."

"I'd like to see him again in six weeks."

"I believe one of you is the murderer!"

"You can make an appointment out front."

"It's a joke, for Christ's sake! Don't you know when you're being kidded?"

In the car, Vivian and Steve continued their conversation.

"We should at least check out Shady Arms," Steve said.

"No," Vivian said, "He has the means to hire a caregiver and live in his own home as long as he wishes. We could fix up the first floor study as his bedroom so he doesn't have to use the stairs.

"I'm not moving downstairs," Clay said, but no one seemed to notice.

"We could put up some kind of gate to keep him from wandering upstairs."

"You mean like they use for toddlers." Steve glanced at the clock on the dash. "Mind if I just drop you guys off and not come in? They're probably waiting for me at the first tee."

"You should take grandpa with you to the course some time. He could ride in the cart. Get some fresh air."

"Sure thing. Hey, Clay, would you like to go golfing sometime?"

"No."

"You'll love it," Vivian said.

"I'll hate it."

"You're going."

After Steve dropped them off, Vivian inspected the downstairs study and declared that it would make an ideal bedroom for Clay. Plenty of space, plenty of sunlight. And it already had a large closet.

What she didn't know was that Clay had put in that closet. It had been so long ago that the paint matched and it was almost impossible to tell the room had been remodeled. Clay had fixed it up years before Vivian had been born as a sick room for his wife after her bone cancer made it too difficult for her to climb the stairs. By that point there was no chance of recovery, so the sick room was more like a death room. She was just returning home to come to grips with the end and squeeze out a few days with Clay and their college-age daughter. Too bad their daughter, Vivian's mom Gwen, rarely found the time to visit. It was the 1970s and she was too busy partying at Villanova to make the trek home more than twice. At that, she didn't stay the night, claiming she had to book it because she was literally swamped with homework. His wife didn't want to be left alone in the downstairs study, so Clay had the hired nurse sit with her while he read detective stories upstairs or listened to the ballgames on the verandah. Before he went to bed, after the nurse left for the day, he tried to pay her a visit. Maybe even plump her pillow. Most nights he simply ignored her, but one night stood out. It would come to mind constantly after the wall came down and Clay was flooded with memories.

Clay had not actually entered the room. Just poked his head in.

"I'm still here. Disappointed?" His wife's eyes had retreated deep into their sockets.

"You need anything before I go to bed?"

"I could use some consideration."

"You want me to turn out the light?" Without waiting for an answer, he stepped in to turn off the lamp on the bedside table.

"Lousy bastard. You never were any good."

"That's right. Sleep tight."

"I don't want to sleep tight. I want to die."

"That's just the pain talking. Good night."

"That's me talking. In pain. I can't do it myself, Clay. I want to die. Kill me."

"'Night."

"It's not like it's against your principles."

Clay closed the door behind him.

Yes, Clay had remodeled the downstairs study. He had put in the closet. And when his wife finally passed, he took out the hospital bed, returned the books, the desk, and the bar, and hardly set foot in the room again. Now his granddaughter wanted him to move in, as if he needed help dredging up bad memories. The medication failed to stop the regrets. They continued to come in waves, and now Clay found himself sitting uneasy in a hotel easy chair covered in sticky notes, wondering why he was sitting in a hotel easy chair covered in sticky notes.

8

There was a murder to solve, a puzzle to fit, and as long as Clay kept the task in mind, he found that he was able to sort through the past while managing to keep the regrets at bay. Somewhat, anyway.

Barrett: Murder victim. The Three Musketeers. Why were they important, and who were they again? There was … Clay, Chuck, and Johnny. Johnny was the new kid. Everybody thought his dad was out of town looking for work, but his grandfather had set Johnny straight, and Johnny had told Clay and Chuck. His dad actually had a job. He worked for the Communist Party as an organizer, a rabble-rouser. His line of work was to foment trouble.

"So are you a Communist, too?" Clay asked on the playground the day he and Chuck became friends with Johnny.

"Are you kidding? I hate the damn Commies. They killed my mother."

"That sounds like something a Communist would say," Chuck said. "They're tricky that way."

61

"So don't believe me."

"We believe you," Clay said.

"Who cares if you do or not? I don't need you. I don't need nobody."

Clay asked Johnny if he'd like to come to his house after school, and Johnny finally agreed after making sure they both knew that he was perfectly happy to be by himself for the rest of his life. When Clay opened the picket gate to the corner lot on which the rectory sat and Johnny looked up at the rambling, gothic house that Clay called home, he was clearly impressed. The rectory seemed like a mansion compared to the narrow row houses he described growing up in Southwark or his grandfather's ramshackled house that hadn't seen a coat of fresh paint since Dewey sailed into Manila Bay.

"Who'd you have to kill to get this joint?" In awe, Johnny looked from gable to gable.

"Comes with the job."

"Not bad. Maybe I should start going to church." And that Sunday he did. The son of a Communist, in fact, became a regular churchgoer.

Clay did what he was told and made friends with Chuck and Johnny, but it didn't seem to make much difference to his parents. The Reverend and Mrs. White remained concerned about his soul.

So there it was. Clay, Chuck, and Johnny became friends for no particular reason. Three became one. They ate lunch at school together, played at recess together, attended Sunday School together, and sat at the back of the sanctuary together to hear Clay's father preach. Three became one. They were together so much that The Rev called them the Three Musketeers.

Mostly the boys played at the rectory. Occasionally they spent time at Chuck's house, but his bedroom was so small and cluttered there was no room to play, just sit among the broken toys, discarded comic sections of the newspaper, and a stack of pornographic stock certificates. Chuck's parents weren't intrusive at least, never having much to say to Chuck or his friends.

And then there was Johnny. The boys never spent time at his grandfather's house, a fact mentioned one day by Chuck who raised such a fuss that Johnny finally relented, and after school one day when he knew his grandfather would be out they paid a visit.

Johnny opened the front door and began to conduct a cursory tour. "There's a coat rack. There's a rug. There's a lamp. And over there is . . . my pop."

Rising from a chair in the living room was a tall, gaunt figure who turned to face the boys. Sunlight from the window behind turned him into a silhouette. The rays flickered through the brush of his crew cut and the curve of his winged ears. As he stepped closer, Clay could see that his cheeks were hollow, his teeth rotting.

"Hey, spud," he said. "Who are your friends?"

Johnny didn't answer.

"I'm Johnny's dad. Good to meet you." He reached out to give Clay a soft, clammy handshake, and did the same with Chuck, who for once had little to say.

"You treating my boy right?" It was an innocent enough question, and it was said in a quiet voice with a smile to back it up, but it still sounded sinister.

"Yes sir."

"You boys learning much at school?"

63

"Yes sir."

"They teaching you about this great country of ours?"

"Yes sir."

"They teaching you about the Haymarket riots?"

"No sir."

"I didn't think so."

Johnny's Dad now turned to Chuck. "Shame what happened to them girls at the Triangle Shirt Waist factory, huh?"

"The what?"

"All the doors locked and the girls they couldn't get out when the fire started."

"What fire?"

"Dozens of them shirtwaist girls jumped to their death. I bet they taught you all about that in school, am I right?"

"What?"

"There's a lot they don't teach you in school, boys. You got to keep yourselves an open mind. Ask questions."

"Can I ask you a question, sir?" Chuck said.

"What's that?"

"Are you . . . are you . . . are you on the lam?"

Johnny's father smiled. "Maybe I am. Maybe I always will be. I got me a meeting up in Tower City I got to get to. I was just passing through and wanted to make sure you were settled into your new school, son."

"I'm fine," Johnny said. "You can go."

"All right then, fellows. We'll see you down the road. I'll be the guy asking questions of the traffic cop. I'll be the guy saying no to the judge. I'll be the guy holding the head of the guy who's had his skull bashed in by a Pinkerton. I'll be the guy —"

"— who's late to Tower City, Pop."

The boys did not play at Johnny's house again. Instead, they kicked around town or holed up in Clay's room. The Reverend and Mrs. White were more than willing to leave them alone, but if given the chance it seemed like Johnny tried to catch their attention. At first, Clay thought Johnny was just hoping to wrangle a dinner invitation. Clay had to admit that his mother always provided a nice table, but after awhile it became so obvious that Johnny actually liked Clay's parents that even Chuck noticed. He teased Johnny about it, accused him of being a cuckoo bird who wanted to kick Clay out of his own nest. Johnny didn't answer back, just turned quiet for the rest of the afternoon. Later, when Clay's mother asked Johnny if he'd like to stay for dinner, he declined the invitation, saying his grandfather was expecting him.

9

Clay peeled off the Post-It note with "The Three Musketeers" written on it and exchanged it with "Stoller." Why was Stoller so important? For that matter, what did an old job have to do with what was happening now?

"Your coffee's getting cold." Clay glanced up to see his granddaughter. For a moment he saw the girl at the roadhouse, Lynne, the one he had saved from a masher that night after the movies. Here was a lead to pursue. Lynne. She was somehow tied into this dizzy affair. After they had a spat and he drove off, Clay remembered circling back to tag after her, then writing down the address where she lived. The next day, he picked up her trail but this time with a palm-size camera in his jacket pocket. He snapped a shot of her leaving the house. Snapped one of the peroxide blonde stepping into the roadster. Clay followed the ladies to Strawbridge & Clothier, where he got out and followed them through the store, taking an occasional picture. A couple hours in, Clay was cupping the camera after taking a shot when he felt a hand on his shoulder.

"Walk with me." The voice came from a beefy guy wearing a double-breasted pinstripe suit. One of his sleeves was empty, folded up, and sewn tight to his shoulder.

"What are you, a store detective?" Clay pocketed the camera.

"What are you, a private op?"

"I asked first."

"Let's go. We don't want to disturb the ladies."

Clay followed the guy to a stairwell. He held out his one good hand. "Hand over the camera."

"What camera?"

"Now you're playing me for dumb. Just give me the camera and beat it."

"What if I don't? You gonna wrestle it away?"

"No, I'll have you arrested, then use some pull on the force to get your license revoked, and if that ain't enough, I can see a tumble down a flight of jailhouse stairs in your future. You shouldn't be so clumsy."

"You want me to just take out the film?"

"No, I want the camera. And the film."

Clay tossed the camera, the kind of underhand flip Granny Hamner made to Goliat at second for the Phils. "I never liked this thing anyway. German made."

The guy caught the camera and rolled it around in his hand to inspect. "Good model. I used to have one just like it."

"Back when you were an op yourself? Before the war took that wing?"

"Something like that."

"Europe or the Pacific?"

"Anzio. You can go now. I've got other business to attend to."

Clay dropped the girl, drove to Pembroke's estate and soon saw the guy leaving in his sports car. Clay followed Pembroke to a horse farm and watched him from a hillside as he inspected some foals, then followed him to the Merion Country Club. Clay talked his way inside the gates long enough to see Pembroke greeting his playing partners for an afternoon round of golf. He watched the foursome on the practice green, saw them tee off. Everybody but Pembroke was a fat duffer in a clown suit. He was the one with the neatly pressed tweeds, the slim silhouette, the smooth backstroke, arrow-straight drive, and picture-perfect follow through.

At the end of the round, Clay was at the country club gates waiting for Pembroke. For a member of the idle rich, the guy sure kept busy. Clay followed him to a downtown hotel for drinks with more yahoos, followed him to Palumbo's in South Philly. That was hardly a surprise. Everybody went to Palumbo's. All the top performers in the country, the likes of Joey Bishop, Mario Lanza, Rosemary Clooney, and Frank Sinatra played Palumbo's. All the politicians curried favor with Frank Palumbo, who knew everybody and whose blessing was required for any serious Philadelphia political career. Mobsters also liked to do business at Palumbo's because the phones weren't tapped. Friendly judges saw to that.

Pembroke and his party stayed at Palumbo's past ten o'clock. Clay then tailed them to a quiet row house. A few minutes later, Pembroke emerged alone, apparently having left his companions well taken care of with some girls for hire. Clay followed his mark to a more remote part of South Philly. It was around midnight when Pembroke got out of his car at a boarded-up worksite. Pembroke smoked a cigarette and paced, occasionally peeking through the plywood barriers, until a sedan pulled up. Out stepped the guy with the Houndstooth hat from the other day at the road house. The conversation between the two didn't last long. Houndstooth was still agitated. Pembroke seemed unsympathetic, finally poking the guy in the chest to make his point with the hand that held a cigarette, causing orange flecks of ember to drift to the sidewalk. Pembroke then returned to his sports car and drove away, leaving Houndstooth standing alone on the quiet street.

He didn't remain alone for long. As he stepped into his sedan, another car down the block turned on its lights, pulled away from the curb, and drove up alongside Houndstooth's ride and stopped. Somebody leaned across the front seat, rolled down the window, and exchanged some words with Houndstooth. Then he slipped out of his car, a small guy in a bright gold jacket, the kind with no lapels. A uniform. He had what looked to be a road map in a white-gloved hand. The other hand was in his jacket pocket. As he bent over Houndstooth's open window, the guy pulled a pistol from the pocket and stuck it in Houndstooth's face. Seconds later, he was receiving a pistol from Houndstooth through the window, and he didn't waste any time turning that gun on its owner. The street was illuminated by a flash, followed a moment later by a sharp crack of a fired revolver and the blare of a car horn that wouldn't quit. The small man in the gold jacket and white usher gloves then leaned in through the window, pulled the body off the horn, arranged things, and calmly circled around the front of his sedan, got in, and drove away. No hurry. No panic. No problem. Clay tried to follow the shooter, but he didn't want to drive by the soon-to-be crime scene, and by the time he negotiated a detour, the other car was nowhere in sight.

The next afternoon, Clay stopped at a newsstand to buy the evening paper. The morning papers wouldn't have had time to cover the killing in South Philly, so he figured he'd find what he was looking for tucked somewhere in the *Bulletin*, maybe right next to the Laff-A-Day cartoon or that night's television listings for channel 10: "The Alan Young Show," followed by "Truth or Consequences." Instead, he looked no further than the top of the front page, lead story, worthy of a thick headline and important enough to push the latest news on the Atom bomb spy case to the bottom half of page one:

INSPECTOR ELLIS FOUND DEAD: APPARENT SUICIDE ON EVE OF SENATE TESTIMONY

Police Inspector Craig C. Ellis, commander of the police vice squad for ten years, shot and killed himself in South Philadelphia near Broad and Patterson Streets today.

He died hours prior to his scheduled appearance as a witness before the Senate subcommittee investigating rackets.

Ellis shot himself in the head with his .32 caliber service revolver and left a suicide note.

The note was written on the back of his pay check and left on the front seat of his car where the shooting took place in the early morning hours. It said:

"I have failed as a leader. My wife did not know of my laxity. I suppose my pain has made me mad. I pray God will help anyone I have caused regret."

Director of Public Safety Samuel H. Rosenberg, who released the text of the note, said Ellis had a heart ailment and believed he had cancer.

Clay read all about the stunned Mayor, the Superintendent of Police, the grieving wife. They said there was no chance that Ellis himself had been involved in anything illicit, but sources reported that the senators wanted to ask Ellis about an anonymous letter they received concerning a country home he owned in another state, and Senate testimony had already revealed a considerable amount of corruption within the vice squad. Of course, no one held Ellis responsible for the actions of others or for the way business had been done in Philly for a very long time.

Clay returned to South Philly to the place the locals called The Neck and the scene of Ellis' reputed suicide. By now, the saw horses the police used to keep away onlookers had been removed. It was just another busy South Philly construction site. As he drove past, Clay could see men stepping down from bulldozers, dropping shovels, peeling off work gloves, and talking among themselves as they headed for the gate. Clay parked his Dodge and walked over to the site, where men with lunchboxes in hand were now scattering. All he learned was that the city had shut down the job. No one knew why for certain. On a placard nailed to the plywood fencing Clay read that on this site would one day stand the new home of the Hosiery Club of America, Inc. He wrote down some permit numbers, and a half hour later he was at the hall of records near City Hall, talking to some lady behind a counter.

"I want to know about an abandoned job site. I want to know why it was abandoned." Clay laid on the counter a slip of paper with the permit numbers. Under it was a five dollar bill.

The lady looked at the fin. "What's this supposed to be?"

"My appreciation for your help."

"We don't get appreciated no more. Not since they sat the grand jury and the Senators come to town." She left the money on the counter but took the sheet of paper. She returned a few minutes later. "That number's been canceled."

"Any reason why?"

"The city's taking the property. Ever hear of eminent domain?"

"What's the city want with it?"

"Apparently, they need to put in a new street down there."

"They don't need another street down there."

"I said apparently."

"Any idea who gave the order? Some inspector or somebody?"

"Yeah, Bill Ellis."

"He in?"

"I think he's out today. His brother killed himself last night. Maybe you read about it in the papers."

"Yeah, the vice cop. Shot himself at the very spot the city wants to put in a street. Kind of a coincidence, don't you think?"

"I don't think no more. Not since they sat the grand jury and the Senators come to town."

10

Clay had always been a sucker for a good detective story. Now he had two murders to solve. The Barrett kid and Houndstooth. Actually, the Three Musketeers had all been suckers for a good detective story. Even a bad one. Chuck had started it all. One Saturday morning, when Clay and Johnny lay on the floor of Clay's bedroom playing checkers, Chuck arrived with something hidden in his jacket, something he said he found in a wooden soap box in his attic. Chuck removed a dozen copies of *Dime Detective* and *Black Mask* detective story magazines, and handed out copies to Clay and Johnny. Clay remembered his heart racing as he studied the cover of a *Black Mask*. A handcuffed woman wearing a jeweled headband, her hands cuffed together, looked up in horror. She was clearly "The Lady in Handcuffs" promised inside the pages of the magazine.

"Would you take a look at this honey pot." Chuck held up a copy of *Dime Detective*. On the cover, a young woman gripped a pistol, while over her shoulder a green-eyed, leering ghoul peered through a porthole. Presumably this was the illustration for "The Phantom and the Porthole."

"These are the goods, boys! The genuine article. There must be a hundred of them at my house." Chuck tossed several more magazines on Clay's bed. "Who knew the old man was such a bookworm."

Clay knew that what they were doing was wrong, but after only a moment of hesitation gave in. He took up a magazine and began reading "The Lady in Handcuffs." While he had difficulty deciphering the slang and making sense of the story, he was thrilled nonetheless. And hooked. They were all hooked.

At the end of the afternoon, Chuck smuggled home the detective magazines and returned them to the cache in the attic. Whenever he had the opportunity, he dipped in for fresh copies, and the boys continued their secret reading club. Because Clay grew afraid they might get caught at the rectory, they began reading the magazines in an old tree house at Johnny's place. But one Saturday when it was raining, the roof leaked and they were forced to find new quarters. Johnny's grandfather hated visitors, and Clay was not interested in spending the afternoon in the clutter of Chuck's room, so they returned to the rectory.

Clay enjoyed the mystery stories more than ever that afternoon, spiced as they were with the possibility that the Reverend and Mrs. White might burst in at any moment and catch the boys in the act of defiling a temple. They were all so nervous they could hardly read, looking to the door every few seconds, listening for the sound of approaching footsteps. The boys felt like many of the characters in the stories they read. Living on the edge. Running scared. By the end of the afternoon they were exhausted and relieved. And utterly satisfied.

Clay sat in the living room after dinner that evening, reading Bible stories while his father worked his way through the Lancaster newspaper. The tale of Noah and the ark did not compare favorably with the vivid prose of the great C.G. Tanney's "And A Little Child Shall Bleed Them." Neither were the illustrations especially thrilling, bereft as they were of smoking revolvers and gum-chewing curvy molls. Clay failed to hear his mother climbing the stairs and entering his bedroom, but he took notice when she quickly descended and entered the living room with a copy of *Black Mask* hanging like a dead rodent from her pinched fingers.

"I just about peed myself," Clay said, when he told Chuck and Johnny what happened the next day.

"What's this I found in your room?" His mother's voice trembled. On the cover of the magazine she held was a woman wearing a low-cut gown gripping a snub-nose .38 in one hand and a lipstick in the other. Across the table sat a dead man sporting a mustache, tuxedo, and a bullet hole in the middle of his forehead. The skirt was looking up just at the moment she finished writing on the victim's shirt front in blood-red lipstick: "Here lies a rat."

Looking at the cover, Clay was unable to speak, overcome by simultaneous feelings of shock, shame, fear, self-loathing, pride, and boyhood lust.

"What, what's this?" The Rev glanced over the horizon of his newspaper. It took him a moment to

77

comprehend what it was that his wife was waving, and then he allowed the newspaper to fall limp over the arm of his chair. "Oh, dear Lord."

"This is garbage!" Clay's mother pointed to the cover. "Apparently this porn-o-graphic illustration is for 'Flaming Angel.'"

It was. And it was wonderful.

"How dare you bring this trash into the rectory? Who sold it to you, young man?"

"I found it," Clay said, and then in his mind completed the sentence to avoid telling a lie: *I found it … delightful.*

"Smart thinking," Chuck would say later. "Technically you did not fib."

"Why didn't you leave it in the gutter where you found it?" Clay's mother demanded.

"I don't know."

"You don't know!"

"I'm not sure."

"You're not sure!"

"I didn't know what it was."

"It's the handiwork of Satan, that's what it is!"

The Reverend White now tried to restore some order to the moment. "You understand, of course, Clay, that you are one step closer to spending an eternity in Hell. Your body licked by neverending flames. Hounds ripping at your flesh. Fowls pecking at your eyes." The Rev could always be counted on to put things into perspective.

Clay was marched to the backyard. Although full punishment was to be meted out at a later date—after his parents had devoted deeper thought and prayer to the matter–Clay was forced to watch as The Rev put a match to the Flaming Angel.

"The important thing is you didn't rat out your friends," Chuck said.

The incident brought the boys even closer together. If they'd had a pocket knife sharp enough to break skin they would have mixed their blood to make the bond eternal. Three had become one.

Clay stared at a Post-It note that said "Focus." He didn't have time to waste on flaming angels. He had his own mysteries to solve. A dead body in the bathroom. Another one in another time on the streets of South Philly. The second case, although more distant, seemed more compelling at the moment. It was certainly one that Clay found easier to grasp, and he decided to pursue the past at the expense of the present, as he sat in an easy chair plastered with notes that he didn't remember writing to himself.

After the recollection of learning that the dead inspector's brother had brought construction to a halt at the job site where the killing took place, Clay remembered he visited another floor at the Hall of Records to learn that the Hosiery Club of America, Inc. was located in the Germantown section of Philadelphia. He drove to the address and found the company housed in a former shirt collar factory, at least according to the faded paint job on the side of a brick wall. It was a small factory-warehouse that had a loading dock more appropriate for dray horses and wagons than modern trucks. When Clay entered the building, he found the doorway crammed with bins of manila envelopes, stacked head-high on top of each other and ready for the post. Only when the receptionist asked if she could help him did Clay spot a girl surrounded by towers of outgoing mail.

"You people look like you could use a little more room." Clay held out a pack of Wrigley's, the top peeled off.

"Tell me about it." She took a stick of gum, paying for it with a smile.

"Don't you got a new place under construction?"

Before the girl could answer, Clay heard a familiar voice say, "Hey Margie." A man approached the reception desk. "I'm expecting a call. Make sure you find me."

The voice came from a man wearing a chocolate brown suit. One of the sleeves was empty, folded and sewn at the shoulder. The guy recognized Clay the moment Clay recognized him.

"Change jobs?" Clay asked. "Don't care for department store work?"

"Maybe you're not such a bad op after all." The man offered his hand as if Clay had an appointment. "Name's Ryan. Let me show you around the place."

And so Clay was given a tour of the Hosiery Club of America. HCA. He saw the knitting machines, the shipping area and its honeycomb wall of large slots to accommodate the different stocking sizes, the clerks who filled the orders and prepared the mailers, and the account clerks with their one-armed adding machines and ledgers. Everyone was piled on top of the other, like the mailers out front. Even Ryan's small office was commandeered for storage. After the tour was over, Ryan had to remove a box of office supplies from a side chair to give Clay a place to sit.

"What's a guy like you doing in the stocking trade?" Clay asked.

"Fixing to make a boatload of money." Ryan manipulated a fresh pack of cigarettes, rapping it on the desk before tearing open one corner and easing out a butt—all performed one-handed and smooth with practice. "An old Army buddy of mine from Philly started the business. I figured he was crazy when he got into the hosiery racket. He thought the same thing about me trying to make it as a Hollywood snoop with just one wing. Turns out he was right and I was wrong."

"How's that?"

"Jack Hess, my buddy, figured out a sweet angle. Strictly on the level and lawyer-approved. We sell stockings through the mail. I mean, nylons. And only the best."

Ryan thumbed open a lighter and put flame to a Camel. Judging by the rasp in his voice and the dead soldiers in the ash tray, Clay estimated that was one of about 50 smokes for the day. "Jack and me actually got our start in Italy during the war. Trading Hershey bars and stockings for a little bit of feminine companionship. Then we did some black-market stuff with parachutes. That's where all the nylon went during the war. So he figured why not give nylon stockings a try stateside? I didn't get it then. I do now."

"There's money to be made in nylons?"

"Plenty. But it's all in the execution. You see, you offer the first pair free but you send three. The ladies mail in a coupon from a magazine—and we only advertise in the best, *Ladies Home Journal, McCall's,* that kind of rag. You bill them for the two extra, then you start mailing two pairs each month along with a bill. To stop the merchandise from coming, the housefrau has to notify us. In writing. It's all in the fine print on the coupon. Jack hired lawyers who specialize in coupon fine print. And if the lady decides not to pay us, we convince her otherwise."

"I get the feeling that's where you come in."

"Collecting's my beat, sure. The threatening letters. The nasty phone calls. When I'm through, trust me, the skirts want to settle up. Maybe it's a lot of trouble for a couple bucks, but word gets around that we mean business. The thing is, though, a lot of our customers like having the nylons come in the mail. It's convenient. No fuss. And Jack makes sure we mail them a quality product. If you give the customer crap and then dun them like hell you're more likely to attract undue attention. But like I said, HCA is completely legit. I'm in on the ground floor and liking my prospects. So I don't need any entanglements right now."

"What entanglements?"

"My wife Phyllis. Her wild step daughter. Our wild step daughter. You're already familiar with the ladies that shop. And then there's you, watching them buy their intimates. My wife spotted you right away and called me. Maybe you're just a deviant. Or maybe somebody hired you. Like maybe the little girl's suspicious husband."

"A man's gotta work."

"You could always put in an application with HCA. We're hiring. You can see, we're busting out at the seams."

"I like working for myself."

"I thought you were supposed to be working for your client?"

"Is that how you did it in Hollywood, Ryan?"

"Sure. I never thought about myself. If some dame I was checking up on for her jealous old man, for instance, asked me to throw in with her and knock him off so we could split the guy's dough and move to Key West, I would have reported the conversation to my client. Pronto."

"Key West is nice, I hear. Especially when it's snowing up north."

"Sure it is. But the only way to get there is the Overseas Highway. It's long and a narrow pike, and who knows what can happen to a fellow along the way."

"You can always take a boat."

"Accidents happen on boats, too. You could fall off and drown. It's been known."

"What if you know how to swim?"

"Nobody can swim with a sack of hammers tied to their ankles."

"Key West isn't the only place in the world."

"True. But accidents have a habit of following around certain dames."

Ryan dipped into a side drawer of his desk and pulled out a cellophane-wrapped envelope. "Here's a sample of the merchandise. Make some gal happy. Some gal you haven't met yet. It's top-drawer stuff. Hey, I bet you didn't know the guy who invented nylon came from

Philly. A DuPont scientist. Probably didn't understand how important the stuff would become. Killed himself in some hotel in town back in '37. A lot of that going around. Suicide. How about that Inspector that blew his top in South Philly last night?"

"Yeah. I heard that on the radio. Funny thing is he did it outside where you're going to build your new plant."

Ryan tapped off the ash of his cigarette. "Just who are you, anyway?"

A man in shirt sleeves and a tie popped into the doorway with a light blue sheet of paper in his hand. "I got another one. Just now." While eying Clay, he passed the paper to Ryan. This must be Hess. Judging by his paunch and baggy eyes, he looked to be about 10 years older than Ryan.

"This is Clay White," Ryan said "He hasn't said so, but I think he's angling for a job."

"Yeah? What's your present occupation if you got one?"

"Discreet enquiries," Clay answered.

"A private dick, huh? Good. Show him the letter. Let's get his take on it."

Clay glanced at the letter all typed in capitals. MOVE TO THE NECK AND YOU CUT YOUR THROAT. "Seems like someone doesn't want you down in South Philly."

"The community's embraced us. We're bringing jobs. Construction jobs now and other ones later. I figure everybody should be happy. Hell, I'm paying to keep everybody happy."

"Maybe they're just crank letters. From some lady who didn't like the stockings you sent her."

"That's what I wondered. Until the city put a stop to our construction. What's our discreet operator think about that?"

"Maybe somebody wants to shake you down." Clay handed the letter back to Hess.

"I'm already good with the Italians. Ida and his boys got their share of no-show jobs on the project. I talked to Reginelli and he doesn't know what the problem is."

"The Jewish mob wouldn't be making a play in that part of town. And Nig Rosen would be lying low right now, what with the Senators and the grand jury."

"Hire this guy, Ryan. I want to know who's behind this shit." Hess left the office.

"So you want a job? Maybe even permanent work with HCA?" Ryan asked.

"Harassing housewives nine to five?"

"Whatever needs to be done in terms of security."

"Sorry, I got a client already. And I don't think I'm the permanent employee type."

"I know. I wasn't either. But we all get old and someday you can't take the rough-and-tumble life of an op." Ryan opened a drawer and removed Clay's camera. "Trust me, you don't want to wait until your future ain't what it used to be." He shoved the camera across the desk. Clay caught it on his lap. Two-handed like Hamner.

11

Clay took up a pen and Post-It pad and wrote "HCA." He stared at the letters and said them aloud.

"I'm sick to death of HCA," said his granddaughter.

"What do you know about HCA?"

"If it wasn't for HCA, Barrett would still be alive. Maybe even Steve. If it wasn't for that stupid company there wouldn't be anything to fight over."

Clay now remembered that his granddaughter's husband, Steve, had inherited HCA. The Hosiery Club of America, the house that Jack built. How could Clay forget HCA? He had devoted countless hours sitting in a conference room as a member of the HCA board of directors, rubber-stamping the decisions of Jack Hess or whoever was chairing the meetings after Jack died. An old black and white newspaper crime scene photo came to mind. It showed Jack Hess and his wife Candy riddled with bullets in the front seat of their Cadillac, heads flopped on their shoulders. It looked like just another one of those mob-hit still photos from the fifties, but the cops insisted this was no contract killing.

The way they saw it, Jack and Candy Hess were driving to South Philly to satisfy one of his periodic urges for authentic Italian food when he made a wrong turn into a bad neighborhood and got shot by some negro teenagers. Of course Jack had lived in the city all of his life, had been driving that same route from Radnor to South Philly a couple times a month for years, and no negro teenager with any sense would venture into an Italian stronghold like South Philly. But some kids confessed to the crime. In Philly they always did, and that was more than enough for the authorities.

Jack Junior inherited control of HCA. He was too young to lead the company, but fortunately his father's old Army pal Paul Ryan was there to run things for him. It was Ryan who delivered his old friend's eulogy at the double closed-casket funeral following the shooting. Clay remembered how with tears in his eyes and a knot in his throat, Ryan told those gathered how he owed everything to Jack Hess, including his life. Ryan had lost his arm in Italy during the war, but it could have been worse if Jack hadn't risked his own skin and dragged him to safety in full view of a German sniper.

"Another five minutes and they would have been etching my name on a marble cross," Ryan said. "After the war when I was having trouble finding work, it was Jack Hess who gave me a job. Together we built HCA, but Jack was the one with the big idea. He could have hired a million guys more qualified than me, but he didn't. He gave his old pal a break."

The funeral wasn't the first time Clay had heard the story about how Jack had saved Ryan's life. At practically every HCA board meeting, Hess made a point of bringing it up, in passing or rendered in full detail. HCA board meetings allowed Hess to command the stage. The meetings were nothing more than a show because Hess controlled the vast majority of the company's stock. Any votes the board took were mere formalities. Clay recalled sitting in the corporate board room in a high-backed leather chair that was more appropriate for a Fortune 500 corporation than some Philly mail order company. The lobby was also filled with artwork bought by Candy Hess and regularly rotated to their home. She picked out the conference room furniture, too. Clay didn't care for the art, but he had to admit the chairs were comfortable. If it wasn't for Hess, Clay would have likely nodded off.

Jack Hess kept the board meetings lively. He didn't need to be drunk, although he usually slugged his way through an afternoon beforehand. He was just naturally entertaining. And abrasive.

"Come on, Ryan," Hess said at more than one HCA board meeting. "Tell 'em what really happened on that sunny afternoon in that godforsaken village square in Italy when that sniper opened up."

"Maybe we should just work our way through the agenda."

"You want me to tell it? You want me to tell 'em how after that Nazi picked off Murphy you panicked and ran? How all you managed to do was get yourself shot and lay there on the cobblestones bleeding like a lanced pig and crying like a little girl?"

"It's an old story, Jack. Maybe we can give it a rest."

"You guys really want to know why I saved his life?

He still owed me fifty bucks from craps." Hess always laughed at this part, and everybody on the board offered a courtesy chuckle.

"Feel like rolling the bones tonight, Paul, just like the old days?"

"No, Jack. I would like to get through the agenda at a reasonable hour."

That was usually when someone on the board made the foolish mistake of letting Hess catch him glancing at his watch.

"You gentlemen got somewhere to go? I guess you pulled them all to your side, huh Paul? Some thanks I get. All of you have it pretty cushy on my dime. You show up a few times a year and get paid pretty good for your trouble. You're nothing but window dressing. When I call the tune, you fuckers dance. You don't like the way we do business here at HCA? It offends your delicate sensibilities? Then why do you cash those checks with HCA printed on 'em?"

Under Jack Junior, the meetings were quicker and stuck to the agenda. Although he was the chairman and sat at the head of the table, it was old reliable Ryan who conducted the meeting as HCA's president. Jack Junior trusted him implicitly, and essentially did whatever Ryan told him to. Jack Junior never pretended to be a businessman. He and his wife, the beneficiaries of inherited wealth, had other interests to indulge. They liked breeding dogs and horses. There were few things that money could not buy, but one of them was the ability of his wife to give birth. Because they both wanted children, they decide to adopt. Clay wasn't aware of all the details, but somehow Jack Junior and his wife adopted a boy from Hungary or Poland. At any rate, it was a Communist country and according to rumor, the infant was smuggled out. In honor of his wife's family, they named him Barrett. The same Barrett whose non-Hess blood now collected in a Center City hotel suite bathroom.

"Did Barrett have gypsy blood?" Clay asked his granddaughter.

"What?"

"He was always on the wild side."

"I wouldn't know."

Regardless, Barrett didn't really work out for the Hesses, but they couldn't very well return him. That was the problem when you took in a stray instead of sticking to pure breeds. With a pure breed, you knew what you were getting. There were no surprises. With Barrett there were always surprises. At the age of seven he was caught shoplifting. At 12 he was caught smoking marijuana, and that was enough for Jack Junior and his wife. They looked for another object of their affection and heir to the throne. They found an American-born baby to adopt. More importantly, they were able to confirm that the mother and father of the child came from well-to-do families from Newport, Rhode Island. The parents were both too young to raise the child, and both their families were eager to avoid an abortion and pretend that this indiscretion never occurred. It was a perfect solution for all involved.

Jack Junior and his wife named the boy Steven for no particular reason. They just liked the name. And they loved the boy who would one day die from a bee sting while playing golf. He was everything that Barrett was not. His parents were so pleased that when he was 12 they bequeathed HCA to him as a bar mitzvah gift. Barrett missed the party for his younger brother. He had been drifting from college to college, enjoying a movable feast of drinking, drugs, and skipped classes. A few weeks after his brother's bar mitzvah, Barrett was presented with a lump-sum amount of money. It wasn't so much his inheritance as it was a severance package. As far as Jack Junior and his wife were concerned, they had settled their obligation to the stray. Barrett didn't seem to mind. He signed every paper placed before him and didn't bother to leave a forwarding address or phone number.

"Barrett was gone for years until his parents died," Clay said to his granddaughter.

"It was a horrific accident."

If not horrific, it was certainly suspicious. Jack Junior and his wife died on the Jersey turnpike. The lug nuts on one of the wheels of their Audi came free, causing a tire to career down the highway. Jack Junior lost control and the car was paddled like a ping pong ball between a pair of speeding semis before flipping over and spinning off into the dark of the night. Steve was just twenty at the time and beginning his junior year at Villanova when he learned about the accident. No one knew how to reach Barrett to tell him about the death of his adoptive parents, but in the middle of the funeral he showed up with his Dominican boyfriend, Raul.

"Raul." Just the sound of his name made Clay smile. "Remember Raul?"

"Not really, no."

Rather than join the other grieving family members, Barrett passed down the receiving line shaking their hands like some business associate, fellow country club member, or neighbor. Raul didn't even bother, exiting through a side door to smoke a cigarette and wait for Barrett outside.

Barrett lingered in Philly for a few days. He saw Steve twice, the second time leaving town with a check in his pocket. Everyone thought that was the last they would see of him or Raul. They were right about Raul, at least.

12

Boxes within boxes within boxes to remove, open, and remove. Clay was no better now at solving mysteries than he had been as a kid. Back then, of course, he made little attempt to piece things together. He often paged back in the magazine to remind himself who did what, when, and why. In the end, it always came down to one thing. A dead guy on the deck. Or in this case, a dead guy on a tile bathroom floor in a Center City Philadelphia all-suites hotel. Some punk named Barrett. Some adopted gypsy punk.

Clay wrote "gypsy" on a fresh Post-It note and pressed it to the left side of the Lazy Boy mixed in with other miscellaneous clues. He had never been good with clues. Of course, when the Three Musketeers read their detective stories back in the day, they had other matters on their minds. After Clay got caught by his parents with a copy of *Black Mask,* the boys had vowed to never again read a detective magazine—at least not until they worked their way through the stack in Chuck's attic. What they failed to consider was that Chuck's father continued to buy new detective pulps and toss them in the crate in the attic, thus ensuring that the boys never exhausted their supply of reading material. The boys also agreed to never read in Clay's bedroom, but this promise was soon violated as well. At first it was simply a matter of convenience; the weather was rotten and the thought of spending the afternoon in Chuck's bedroom simply intolerable, but they quickly realized that the chance they might be caught by Clay's parents provided a irresistible thrill. The tension in the room was now ten times greater than before Clay's mother had found a magazine. So delicious was the taste of forbidden fruit that even the most tepid tale of mystery, offering wooden characters, threadbare situations, creaky dialogue, half-baked plot turns, and resolutions that even nine-year-old boys found strained was rendered lyrical in language, elegant in plot, and thought-provoking in theme. Clay getting caught was perhaps the best thing to happen to literature since Guttenberg. Or the paperback.

The Reverend and Mrs. White took their time in determining an appropriate punishment for Clay. A week after the incident with the Flaming Angel, Clay was playing cards in his room with Johnny and Chuck when he was pulled away by his mother and led to the dining room dominated by a large reproduction of Da Vinci's "The Last Supper." While the future disciples discussed among themselves who was destined to betray Jesus, or were perhaps just grumbling about the food, Clay was informed that he was about to hear his sentence.

The Reverend White was already seated at the head of the table praying quietly to himself when Clay and his mother took their usual places. Clay could see the shoes of Chuck and Johnny on the stairs as they listened in. The Rev looked up, waited until Clay bowed his head in shame, and declared but one word. "Baseball."

"You're going to play baseball, learn teamwork, and do what the coach tells you to," his mother said.

"I believe the leaders are called managers. Sounds rather industrial but there you have it."

At least Clay had the other musketeers for company. Chuck's parents decided he too could benefit from a team sport and maybe lose some baby fat. One Saturday morning, Clay and Chuck walked together to the municipal diamond for their first baseball practice. They found Johnny waiting for them, sitting on the bench lined up between home and first base.

Yes, three had indeed become one. Clay, Chuck, and Johnny now spent almost all of their time together. The same class at school, on the playground together at lunch and recess, then baseball practice, and finally at church on Sunday. They sat in the back row of pews in the corner where Chuck searched through the concordance of his Bible and paged to any passage with "ass" in it or the mention of anything remotely sexual.

One Sunday, Johnny didn't attend church, and after Clay had dinner with his parents, he and Chuck walked to Johnny's grandfather's house. Johnny was in the backyard with an old ax handle, tossing crab apples in the air and hitting homers over a barbed wire fence. The end of the handle was wet and stained red.

"Where were you this morning?" Chuck called.

As Johnny put a finger to his lips and urged them to step back, they heard someone in the house exclaim, "Jesus fucking Christ!"

The boys huddled against the side of the house.

"It's my dad," Johnny whispered. "He's been shot."

Before Johnny could stop him, Chuck peeked through a window and was quickly spotted by Johnny's father. "Hey you! Come in here. I want you to see this. Johnny, bring in your friends."

The boys entered the kitchen through the backdoor to find John LeMaster sitting shirtless at the table, while someone with a pair of tweezers removed buckshot from the back of a red and purple shoulder. On the table was a wash basin with several pellets in the belly.

"I want you boys to see your tax dollars at work." LeMaster drank from a tin cup, then refilled it from a bottle of bootleg whiskey. "Fucking cops. There to protect property, not people. People are the problem, you see. And I'm a real big problem. Good thing I was only shot by a riot gun."

"What happened?" Chuck asked.

Johnny punched Chuck in the arm. "What do you think happened, stupid?"

"It's a good question! You boys should be asking questions." LeMaster threw back his whiskey and nodded to the other man to continue picking out buckshot. "The coalminers up in Tower City are getting a pretty raw deal. Always have. That was Molly Maguire territory up there until the Pinkertons infiltrated and blew it all to hell. So we're doing a little organizing to see that the men get their rights. Only the mine owners don't like it. They control the towns, and the towns pin badges on any goon the company says to. Some of those goons broke up our meeting at the Tower City grange. Jesus! Hold it a moment, Tom."

The guy with the tweezers paused. "It ain't gonna get no easier."

LeMaster closed his eyes and bit his lip for a second before letting his friend rejoin the operation. "This one particular goon has it in for me, see. There's always one, although in my case there's five or six. This one, McNulty, isn't satisfied with just chasing us away with a boot to the ass. He fires a load of shot at me. If I had zigged instead of zagged it would have blowed my head off. As it was, it clipped my shoulder."

"Are you going to die?" Chuck asked.

"Everybody dies."

"I mean right now."

"No. I got unfinished business to tend to." LeMaster poured another drink. "Unfinished business up in Tower City."

13

Clay tickled the "HCA" note, then pulled it free and placed it on the chair arm, running his thumb along the top edge to press it in place. He took up his pen and circled the letters, HCA. Everything centered on HCA. Clay was certain this Barrett kid was dead because of HCA. The Stoller case, somehow that too was connected to HCA. A killing had taken place at the HCA job site. It didn't matter how long ago it occurred, Clay had to know why. He remembered standing in the back among the curious at the funeral of Inspector Ellis. Watched half-a-dozen white-gloved cops fire a volley of rifle shots. Listened to a bagpiper squeeze a dirge. All the top city cops were in attendance, wearing their dress uniforms with the polished brass and steamed ribbons. All the big politicians were there as well, including the mayor and the men he hated and feared the most, the reformers Dilworth and Clark. A lot of pomp and circumstance for a guy that was supposed to have bumped himself off on the eve of giving testimony. Maybe, like Clay, everyone knew the suicide story was a little too convenient. Maybe some of them, like Clay, knew it for certain. Standing front and center when Ellis was laid to rest was the widow and the rest of his family, including brother Bill, the building inspector. He was a small, fidgety man with salt-and-pepper hair and a caterpillar mustache.

After the service was over, invited guests gathered for a dinner at a private room at the Bellevue-Stratford Hotel, where Kefauver and the rest of the Senators were also staying and all of Philly's Most High regularly gathered to eat, drink, and deal. Clay stood across the street and watched as the limos of the big guns pulled up to the hotel. The smaller-caliber types drove themselves, and men dressed in bright blue jackets ran up to take the keys, park the cars, and trot back to the front of the hotel for more. When it seemed all the cars were parked and the valets were milling around smoking cigarettes and rolling the guff, Clay crossed Walnut Street and approached three of the men. He asked if any of them knew of a place in town where the valets wore gold jackets with black trim.

"Depends on what part of town, Pally?" The guy who answered was balancing a toothpick in the corner of his mouth.

"South Philly."

"Only one joint in South Philly parks cars in that kind of getup. Picolo's 500 Club."

"Nick Buck's joint?" asked one of the other valets.

"That's the spot. They like to act like they're the 500 in Atlantic City. They're both mobbed up but Picolo's lacks the spit and polish, and they don't got the posh casino in the back with the private entrance like the

Five. They just run numbers and shit. Still, you don't want to cross the Picolo brothers."

After the funeral dinner was over and the valets were scrambling to bring the cars of the guests to the front, Clay sat waiting behind the wheel of his idling sedan parked down the street. He spotted his man, Bill Ellis, and tailed him as he drove away alone. Clay made sure to keep a car or two between them. For quite awhile it seemed like it was the same car separating the two. After ten minutes, Ellis pulled over and flagged down the car. The driver rolled open his window, and Ellis flashed a revolver. The car quickly pulled away, leaving Ellis standing in the street, gesturing wildly at the tail lights. He returned to his own car, but the engine refused to turn over. He kept trying until there was no hope of it starting.

Clay, who had drifted over to the curb and killed his lights to watch, pulled up alongside Ellis, leaned across the seat and rolled down the passenger-side window, just like the guy in the gold jacket had done the other night before he gunned down the Inspector with his own cannon.

"Got a problem?" Even as he asked, Clay had his hand on his door and was beginning to open it. He circled around to the front just as Ellis was stepping out of his own car.

"I guess I flooded the damn thing."

"Nothing to do but open the hood, air it out, and wait." Clay, the Good Samaritan, even unlatched the hood for Ellis. He then reached into a pocket and pulled out a flask. "You look like you could stand a drink."

Ellis shook his head, but quickly changed his mind and accepted the flask, offering a muttered "Thanks" in return.

"I saw you pull that gun."

Ellis spilled whiskey down his chin.

"My guess is you got more than car trouble, brother."

"Who are you? What do you want?" Ellis shoved the flask in Clay's hand.

"I'm nobody." Clay capped the flask and dropped it in a side pocket of his jacket.

Ellis began to pull out his pistol, but before he could clear his coat pocket, Clay caught Ellis by the wrist, kicked him in the shin, and quickly twisted the gun away from him as Ellis dropped to the ground.

Ellis sat on the running board of his sedan, head in hands. "Now what?"

"Have another drink." Clay tapped him on the shoulder with the flask. "And tell me why Craig shot himself."

"Are you a cop?"

"No."

"You're a Senate investigator or working for the Grand Jury, aren't you?"

"I'm a private op, okay? I don't care about Senator Kefauver or the Special Grand Jury. The interests I represent just want to know why your brother shot himself in front of a work site that the next day you shut down."

"Craig didn't shoot himself. He was murdered."

"That's not the way it's figured."

"Maybe that's the way they want it figured. Nobody needs any complications, right? Certainly no murder investigation. I don't know who wrote that suicide note on his paycheck, but he was murdered all right."

"Why and who did it or arranged to have it done?"

"Probably whoever sent those letters."

"What letters?"

"The ones that told Craig he needed to get me to close down that project in The Neck or certain information would come out."

"Did he ask you to close it down?"

"Sure, but he must have known I couldn't. There were other parties concerned. He knew I wasn't a straight arrow. None of the building inspectors are. He was such a damn boy scout. But I guess he must have made some mistake years ago that could give a person leverage over him. Maybe that's why they made him the head of the vice squad. He could be counted on to do his job up to a point. Maybe somebody else found out about his secret and threatened to tell."

"Is it true like it said in the papers he owned a house in some other state?"

"I don't really know what he could have done that was so bad. He always made me feel dirty. Wouldn't even take a Christmas present from me without making some kind of comment, wondering how I could afford it on my salary. So when he needs a favor, when he wants me to shut down that South Philly job, what do you think I say?"

"I don't know. What do you say?"

"I say, 'I can't do that. That would be dishonest. Good thing you're my brother, or I'd have to report you.'"

"And now after he's dead, you hold up the project. Why?"

"I'm a Goddamn coward. Okay? Whoever killed Craig said they'd kill me, too."

"You got a letter? A threatening letter?"

"Yeah, I got a letter."

"Blue paper?"

"That's right."

"So why are you so nervous now? You did what you were told. Why's a guy like you carrying a gat?"

"I'm double-crossing Ida's crew. I can't win. One side or the other in this isn't going to be happy with me. Maybe one of them sent you."

Clay broke open the pistol and allowed half-a-dozen slugs to pour into his hand. Dropped them in a pocket. Slapped the rod on the roof of the sedan. And walked back to his Dodge.

Clay drove to South Philly and pulled up in front of Picolo's 500 Club. A valet wearing a gold jacket leaning against the wall ditched his cigarette and slowly made his way around to the driver's side of the car, but Clay didn't budge. "You getting out? I'm not in the business of giving out driving directions."

Through the open window, Clay held out a creased five dollar bill between his fingers like a cigarette. "I'm in the market for some information. Was there a kid parking cars here the other night?"

"What's it to you if there was?"

"I found butts in the ash tray that weren't mine. And the mileage was wrong. I'm thinking he went for a joy ride instead of parking my car."

"So?"

"So I want to put a gun to his fucking head and tell him I don't appreciate the disrespect."

"Yeah? Well, I guess the little shit deserves it."

"Who is he?"

"Nicky. Nicky Scarfo. Little Nicky Scarfo. His uncles own this place. The kid parks cars and thinks he's the crown prince."

"Where is he?"

"He got fired the other night, though his Mom will probably get his job back for him soon enough. Seems he disappeared for a good half-hour. Probably taking your ride for a spin."

"Any idea where he might be?"

"It's possible." The guy clammed up until Clay skimmed another bill from his roll. "Atlantic City. He stopped by all dressed to the nines in a canary yellow suit. Said he was going to see the elephant."

"What's that?"

"The 500 Club. Skinny D'Amato's joint. So, you staying or going?"

Decades later, Clay learned all about Atlantic City from books when he wasn't reading his old letters while sitting on his verandah listening to Phillies' games. AC was one of four towns that made up Absecon Island, a long spit of land sandwiched between the ocean and seven miles of marsh hugging the coast of New Jersey. There was no reason for a burg to spring up there, except it was the shortest distance between Philly and the Atlantic Ocean. The town was really just an excuse to build a railroad in the 1850s, somebody's dream to build a resort to rival Cape May. Atlantic City didn't have much to offer, other than a cheap train ride and rapacious insects, until the first temporary Boardwalk was built in 1870. Bigger and better versions followed, and by the turn of the century, Atlantic City's Boardwalk, while not one of the great wonders of history, attracted tourists from around the world to stroll its four miles of wooden planks.

Walking the Boardwalk or riding in rolling chairs held limited entertainment value, but that deficiency was remedied by the rise of vaudeville and entertainment piers, which until they were better constructed had a tendency to float out to sea during rough weather. Of course some men needed a stiffer dose of fun, and so in the dark side streets of Atlantic City flourished saloons, horse rooms, brothels, and even a few opium dens. Atlantic City became a wide-open town, a twenty-four-hour town, a town with a Boardwalk on steel girders where the respectable could show off their finery, and a seamy underbelly where they could slake their thirst and let loose their demons. On the beaches, women showed off their ankles and men in black bathing suits signaled their desires for one another by wearing colorful silk garters. The passage of Prohibition provided Atlantic City with a new business opportunity, as the town's access to the ocean now made it a hub for rum running. Mobsters from New York City and Philadelphia did business in Atlantic City. Making sure everybody was kept happy, including law enforcement, was Nucky Johnson, the town's former sheriff.

Nucky had plenty of friends but he also made one powerful enemy, newspaper mogul William Randolph Hearst. Nucky made the mistake of calling Hearst's mistress, actress Marion Davies, a tramp. With a little prompting from the Feds, Nucky was taken down on tax evasion charges. Replacing Nucky as King of Atlantic City, at least in a social sense, was Skinny D'Amato, who ran the 500 Club. The Five became one of the country's hottest nightclubs, known as the place where Dean Martin and Jerry Lewis launched their act after the war.

When Clay drove from Philly to Atlantic City looking for Little Nicky Scarfo he took the Black Horse Pike, one of the highways President Harding had given to Atlantic City back when Nucky Johnson had pull. Sophie Tucker was appearing at the Five that week. She was always popular with the sporting crowd that filled the club's backroom casino. Too bad Kefauver's committee was in Philly at the time. The casino was shuttered because the Senators were coming to Atlantic City, the last stop for most shows bound for Broadway. It would never reopen and the club had to be remodeled. The Five would have to go completely legit whether it wanted to or not.

Because Labor Day had passed, Clay had no problem finding a place at the bar. The Five was considered a class joint. Only top-shelf hookers were allowed to work its bar. One of them was at Clay's elbow even before his drink arrived.

"Tell me you're from Kansas City." She was all hair, lipstick, fur, gloves, baubles, and mid-priced perfume. "I like men from Kansas City."

"Why's that?"

"Haven't you heard the song? Everything's up to date in Kansas City."

"I heard men from Kansas City are easy to grift."

"There's that, too."

"You want to do something for me?"

"Don't you want to know if I want a drink first?"

"I guess in Kansas City they don't know they're paying for food coloring when they spring for a lady's drink at an AC bar."

"I like you. You're smart."

"You like everybody."

"I say I like everybody. But I really like you."

"I like you, too," Clay said. "I'd like you even better if you told me if you've seen a little guy wearing a canary yellow suit tonight."

"Maybe I have. Maybe I haven't."

"Maybe there's something in it for you. Maybe a fin."

"Maybe a sawbuck?"

"Why not?" Clay reached for his roll. "I'm in Atlantic City. Might as well get clipped."

After she deposited the ten inside a long glove, the chippy said there had been a little kid wearing yellow that came to the bar. He tried to talk up Skinny D'Amato but got the freeze. Skinny didn't waste charm on small timers. The kid was apparently trying to get into the casino and didn't believe that it was actually closed. One of the bartenders told the kid of a private game. The canary was gone about an hour and came back broke, asking the bartender for train fare home to Philly, figuring it was the bartender's fault for getting him into a crooked dice game. Of course the bartender wasn't buying the story and didn't give him anything, so the kid starts asking where the fruits hang out in Atlantic City. Probably, the girl said, he was planning on rolling a queer to raise some cash, figuring a Nancy wasn't going to squeal to the cops.

"So do you know where he might go?" Clay asked.

"But one place," she said. "Snake Alley."

14

"Where are the police?" his granddaughter moaned. "They can't be that busy."

Clay watched his granddaughter lie back on the bed, close her eyes, then turn on her side and draw up her legs. Clay could hear her breathing, deep and steady, and he too slowly closed his eyes. His thoughts drifted off, almost like in a dream but not quite. He was sitting at a booth in a diner, drinking coffee, waiting for someone. He reached into a side pocket of his trench coat and removed a piece of cardboard. It was one half of a box top for Jello. He knew he was waiting for someone he had never met before, someone who held the other half of the box top, someone who would tell him what to do next. Clay looked out the window at dark, rain-soaked streets, empty save for a lone man approaching the diner. His face was hidden under the shadow of his hat brim. He wore a trench coat like Clay, his collar turned up to guard against the cold.

A moment later, the man was standing in the doorway of the diner looking over the clientele. There wasn't much to choose from. A couple of milk truck drivers finishing up their eggs at the counter, about to start their morning run. A hatless sot with grey stubble and sunken cheeks at a booth glaring into an empty cup. And then there was Clay. The man walked slowly in his direction.

"The team looks good this year," he said.

"They're just a bunch of bums," Clay replied.

The man sat down across from Clay. From a pocket, he removed something and laid it on the table. It was half of a box top. Clay removed his share of a box top and placed it along side. The two halves matched perfectly. The man called for coffee and it wasn't until after he was served that he spoke.

"You have a job? You have a room?"

"Yes."

"Good."

"What do I do now?"

The man placed a slip of paper on the table. On it was written an address.

"What's this?" Clay asked.

"A machine shop. The owner needs to be dealt with."

"Who is it?"

"His name doesn't matter. Let's just use the initial 'J.' He doesn't matter."

"Dealt with how?"

"If you need to ask that question, perhaps they sent the wrong man."

Clay reached out for the address. "I understand."

"Good."

"How soon does the work need to be done?"

"Today if possible. Tomorrow by all means."

"Subtlety not required?"

"The result is all that is required. I'll pay for the coffee."

The man began to rise from the booth when Clay caught him by the wrist. "Is that it? No explanation? No reason why?"

"I guess you really were born here. Your kind are all alike. No discipline. Too individualistic. You make too much work for me."

The diner faded away. Clay was now driving in the country with the high-beams on, rain pelting the windshield that was wiped clean every half-second. The next moment, the car pulled off the side of the road, the engine idling, while he trudged through wet autumn leaves, the path illuminated by a bobbing flashlight. After twenty yards or so Clay paused. He focused the light on the ground. At first it looked like more wet leaves but Clay soon made out a shape. A shoe heel. Then a sole of the shoe. Then the ankle of someone whose foot fit that shoe, someone who was clearly dead.

Clay opened his eyes, his head snapping back into the easy chair. He saw a young woman asleep on the bed in front of him. He was in a hotel room, sitting in an easy chair, the arms of which were covered in yellow sticky notes. He didn't bother to read them or question why they were there. He had a more immediate concern. He felt the need to escape that room. He looked around and realized that he had been left alone with a girl and she had fallen asleep. He might never get another chance.

Clay pushed himself out of the chair and softly made his way to the front door. He felt his pockets for the box top. On a small side table near the entrance to a kitchenette, Clay noticed a magnetic key card tucked in a small envelop with the room number written on it, #809. Even though it wasn't a box top, he felt he needed to take it. He slipped the card into the pocket of his windbreaker, then slowly opened the door to the room, eased his way into the hallway, and quietly closed the door behind him.

Rather than risk the elevator, Clay walked briskly to the end of the hallway and a red exit sign. He entered a stairwell and descended two flights before he was out of breath and sat down. He inhaled deeply and closed his eyes. When he opened them again he found himself sitting on some stairs in some building somewhere. Why was he sitting here? He needed to keep moving. That was the only thing of importance. But was he supposed to be going up or was he supposed to be going down? He finally decided he should go down, to get outside on the street to at least learn where he was and get his bearings.

Clay peered down the stairwell through the railings and realized he was in no condition to descend the stairs to the ground floor. Instead, he went down half a flight, made use of an entry door, and walked down a hallway in search of an elevator. Something about the hallway seemed familiar, but really, wasn't it like a thousand other carpeted hallways in a thousand other hotels in his life? What was so special about this one?

Clay paused in front of room 603 and stared at the fisheye in the middle of the door. He raised his hand, brought his fingers together to make a fist, and took a deep breath in anticipation of knocking on the door. Was he ready? Ready for what? He was here, wherever here was, and needed to act. Whatever it was couldn't be put off forever. It had to be dealt with now. All that mattered was the result. Clay rapped on the door and waited.

A moment later, the door swung open. A small man with modest gray hair and thick glasses wearing a powder blue cardigan and a tie answered. "I thought you weren't coming," he said, stepped aside, allowed Clay to enter, and then led him to the main room of the suite. "Please have a seat." The man gestured toward a Lazy Boy. Clay sat down and looked at the arms of the chair. Something was wrong with the chair. Something seemed missing.

The small man sat on the edge of the bed covered in a blood red damask duvet cover. "I just want to make things right."

"Maybe it's too late for that," Clay said.

"The thing is, my wife doesn't know."

"She typed it up."

"Excuse me?"

"She typed up the notes. She's just as guilty as you are."

"I don't understand."

"That's what they'll say, anyway, to put pressure on you. To get you to tell everything you know. We can't let that happen."

"What are you talking about?"

"Don't play dumb, J."

"My name's Harold. And you're —"

"That's not important. If not me, then somebody else will do the job."

"I'm talking about the burial plot."

"I don't care what you call it."

"The pre-need contract I signed. Isn't that why you're here? I told them on the phone it was a silly mistake. I thought my wife would want us to be buried together where she was born. It was supposed to be a 40th anniversary present. I know that may sound strange to some people, but the funny thing is she bought burial plots for the two of us where I was born. Cleveland. So you see I don't need to be buried twice. It's been a terrible mix up and I was hoping I could straighten it out while I was in town."

"You're good."

"I'm just trying to cancel the contract. I understand if there's a termination fee."

There was a knock at the door.

"I don't know who that could be."

"Answer it, but get rid of them," Clay said.

Harold looked puzzled but rose from the bed and walked to the door, peered through the fisheye, and cracked open the door.

"Mr. Markstein?" Clay heard a man say. "I'm Jenkins from StoneMor about the pre-need contract."

A moment later, Jenkins and Markstein were standing in front of Clay asking if he was lost, if he was confused.

"You shouldn't have got involved." Clay told Jenkins.

"Sir, do you know who you are?"

Of course, he knew who he was. He was Clay White, the only son of the Reverend and Mrs. White. He was one of the Three Musketeers. His friend Chuck was the son of a salesman, and his friend Johnny was the son of a labor agitator. They did everything together. They went to school together, attended church together, played baseball together.

Clay ignored Markstein and Jenkins and thought about baseball. Those memories seemed like the most important thing in the world at the moment. Clay remembered the smell of the wool uniforms they were given the day before the first game of the season. They had been stored in a cedar chest all winter and smelled like moth balls. The three boys didn't get into the first game of the season until the last inning when the coach sent the three of them in a row to pinch hit. Clay struck out on three straight pitches, never making an offer. Chuck followed and struck out as well, flailing at every one. Finally, Johnny stepped to the plate. He bit his lower lip and wagged the bat behind his ear waiting for the pitch. He took the first one low. Never taking his eyes off the pitcher, he waited for the next one. When it came in thigh-high over the plate, he stepped forward and slashed the ball into left center, splitting the outfielders for a homerun.

"Atta boy!" the manager yelled.

Johnny quickly became the star of the team. Not only could he hit, he could pitch. He had a knack for throwing the ball down the middle and allowing a natural tail to bring the ball to the edge of the plate, to the black border. All of Johnny's pitches were on the edges. Never down the middle. Always on the edge. On the black.

Jenkins asked Clay if he had any identification on him.

"Who won the game?"

"Maybe we should call the front desk," Markstein said.

Clay pushed himself up from the chair, claimed he felt better, and made his way to the door. The last thing he needed were the authorities. As he hurried down the hallway toward the elevator, Jenkins called after him, "Are you sure you're okay?"

Clay ignored him and quickly punched the down button of the elevator. The car must have been waiting; the elevator doors lurched open immediately. Clay stepped in, selected the lobby button, and waited for the doors to close.

15

Why was Clay in an elevator? Was he going somewhere? Of course, he was going somewhere, and it was urgent that he get there. He just wasn't sure where that was. Perhaps he was meeting someone. Or was he looking for someone? And if he was looking for someone, who? Little Nicky? It had to be Little Nicky. Clay had some more questions for the kid.

Clay remembered the first time he met Little Nicky. He had gone looking for him in Atlantic City in Snake Alley. The first stop of any tour of Snake Alley was the Entertainer's Club, a joint run by a woman named Louisa Mack. She opened the place just after Prohibition came into effect. It was a speakeasy that became a fay meeting place, and after the repeal of Prohibition she kept it relatively anonymous for the sake of her furtive clientele. Clay could still picture it tucked away on a side street, even though there was no sign in front or the long bay window of a typical tavern. A bare light bulb hung over a simple front door of a house that looked like any other in the neighborhood, with the notable exception that it was kept up better. Louisa made sure the sidewalk was swept every day and the house painted each year—yellow with green trim. She also kept a dress code: a jacket and tie after six, even if the temperature on the beach that day cracked 100. The men were also not allowed to dance with one another, and if they kissed, they got tossed. Louisa made sure to go to church on Sunday, despite the late hours she kept the night before, and she sat in the front pew in case subtlety was lost on the locals. But what local really cared? When you chose to live in Atlantic City, you either made peace with the ways of the world or you moved on.

Clay walked the eight blocks from the Five to the Entertainer's Club, located just beyond the colored side of town. At the door was Louisa, who greeted customers and gave them the once-over. She exchanged some pleasantries with a pair of men who arrived just before Clay. They must have been regulars, at least for that week. Louisa was in her 50s, her face peach colored and pasty with makeup. Her grey-streaked hair laced with orchids hung down to her waist.

When Clay stepped in the doorway, Louisa lost the smile. "Can I help you, mister?"

"This is a bar, right?"

"This is my place. These are my friends. I'm not sure this is your kind of place."

"I'm looking for somebody."

"Everybody's looking for somebody."

"A little guy wearing a yellow suit."

"A friend of yours?"

"No. We've never met before." Clay scanned the room beyond Louisa's shoulder. It looked like any other crowded bar, probably more crowded than the rest of the other off-season Atlantic City joints. A lot of cigarette and cigar smoke. A lot of chaotic conversation. A lot of men, and men dressed like women, but few actual women.

"If you've got a badge, maybe now's the time to show it."

"I'm a private op looking for a man for my own reasons, but you might be interested because I'm told he's looking to kick over some of your guests for easy money."

"I got no beefs with ops if they announce their business, but I don't talk about the people who walk through my doors. Luckily, the party you're looking for never made it past me. I sent him away awhile ago. Not our type."

Clay left the Entertainer's Club and searched the side streets and alleys off New York Avenue. It was a quiet night, with the exception of barking dogs, a cat fight, and a guy threatening to kill his wife. Clay approached an alley as a pair of men emerged. One of them dusted off his yarmulke and began pinning it to the back of his head while his friend rubbed the small of his back before pushing his hand through the crook of the other one's elbow. They spotted Clay, dropped their arms, and silently walked away.

Clay paused at the mouth of the alley and scanned its length. Midway down, beyond a garbage can and a busted crate, he spotted a shoe, a sock, the bare flesh of a calf, and a canary yellow pant leg. On the other side of the garbage can he found a small man sprawled on the ground, his hair mussed and one shoulder of his jacket ripped. The kid cracked open his eyes. "Can you give me a hand, buddy?" As Clay pulled him to his feet, the kid said he had just been jumped by five guys.

"What's your name?" Clay asked.

"Nicky. Nicky Scarfo. What's yours?"

"You can call me Mack. You know, like Connie Mack."

Clay treated Nicky to some coffee and a sinker at an all-night diner on New York Avenue and listened further to the story of the five, maybe it was six guys, who circled Nicky and pummeled him. Too bad there was so many of them. He used to box, so it wasn't like one or two of them could have handled him. And you know why they jumped him? Because he was Italian, that's why.

"Maybe they just wanted your dough."

"They could have wanted anybody's dough, but they went after the Italian. It's a sick world."

"You from Philly?"

"Yeah, just in town for a little fun. Some fun."

"You got a way back to town?"

"At least I got my car and I filled the tank when I got to AC. So there's that."

"Tell you what, Nicky. Let's go have some drinks. Some laughs. On me."

And so Clay and Nicky toured some local establishments, but not the Five, had a few drinks along the way, and Nicky began to open up about his life. About his job at his uncle's place, parking cars when he felt he should have been learning how to run the real business. Gambling. Numbers. Bookmaking.

"That's against the law, last I heard."

"You don't say." Nicky threw back a drink, then spread his palms on the table and leaned forward. "There's only one law in the world that matters, Mack. The law of the jungle. This is the jungle. Atlantic City. South Philly's the jungle. In the jungle you're either a lion or you're lion food. And I ain't nobody's Goddamn meal."

"I hear the racketeers run the numbers in Philly. That's what the Senators say in the papers."

"My uncle's a racketeer. That shock you, Mack? I'm gonna be one myself. Hell, I already am one. I've taken care of a few problems. Guys who don't want to back their markers. That sort of thing."

"I thought you parked cars."

"I do what I have to do to pay my dues." Nicky pushed back from the table, crossed his legs, pulled a cigarette from a pack on the table, and tapped the tobacco in place. "So, what's your line?"

"I'm a salesman. A Bible salesman."

"That's just another racket, right?"

"Pretty much."

"You do what you need to do to get the job done, am I right? Let me ask you something, Mack." Nicky lit a wooden match one-handed with his thumbnail. "Ever kill a man?"

"In the service. Probably more than a couple. But not up close."

Nicky put the light to his Pall Mall. "I mean kill a man right in front of you without the law saying it was for the good of the country."

"Have you?"

"Forget I even brought it up."

"Why'd you bring it up?"

"I don't know." Nicky gazed around the room, a contented look on his face as he rolled some smoke in his mouth before blowing a ring. "Life is good."

"Are you telling me you kill people for hire? What do they call that? A button man?"

"Of course not. Nobody's ever paid me to kill nobody. At least not yet."

"Not yet?"

Nicky leaned forward and lowered his voice. "There's this dame. There's always a dame, right? Even in the Bible. You should know. There's always a dame wanting you to bring her some guy's head on a plate. Well, this particular dame wants this particular guy out of the way, see. Only she doesn't say so in so many words, but if you're a smart cookie you get the drift. And if you're a lion like yours truly, you take out the gazelle if that's the smart play."

"So you're saying you knocked somebody off for the sake of a dame?"

"Maybe there's dough involved, too. There's always dough involved."

"Even in the Bible?"

"Sure. Dames and dough. Look it up. Front page, Genesis."

"So who was the particular . . . gazelle?"

"Maybe I said too much already."

"You can't stop now." Clay looked over at the bartender and pointed at Nicky's glass to have it refilled.

While the bartender splashed more whiskey in his glass, Nicky dragged on his cigarette and admired the smoke as it leaked from his nostrils. He tapped some ash onto the floor as the bartender drifted out of earshot. "Funny thing is, I got the wrong guy."

"The wrong guy?"

"It happens. You'd think she'd appreciate the effort at least. But I don't figure she would, so I didn't tell her. Let her read about it in the papers. Thing is, she read the papers, figured it out, and we're through now anyway. Not that I much care, because I don't."

"So, let me get this straight. This dame hints around that she wouldn't be sorry if a certain party makes his exit. And she happens to know where he'll be at a certain hour to meet somebody. Probably some quiet place, I'm guessing. And you show up and powder the wrong guy."

"Not everything always goes according to Hoyle."

"So who was the unlucky bastard?"

Nicky leaned closer. "How did I know it was some kind of cop? It's not like he was wearing a uniform. He just looked like somebody that should be shot. Nobody else in town seems to think so, my uncles included. Good thing they didn't know what really happened. But they took care of it, anyway."

"Who took care of what?"

"Everybody. And I mean everybody took care of it. There's too much heat in Philly right now. I guess it's better for all concerned that it look like the guy done himself in. Good thing I plugged him with his own cannon." Nicky tapped his temple. "Pays to think. I probably said too much already. Maybe I'll have to erase you, too." Nicky laughed and threw back the last of his drink. "Thanks for the party, Mack. Let's keep in touch. Stop by Picolo's some night and I'll stand for the drinks."

Clay walked Nicky to his car. The sun was rising, Snake Alley was finally going to bed, and Louisa was probably ready to hose down the sidewalk.

A chime startled Clay. He was in an elevator, the doors of which were now admitting a young woman, who smiled at him. She was about to press the lobby button but refrained since it was already lit. Clay must have pressed the button. He must be on his way to the lobby. They rode together the final three floors, the doors opened, and the woman exited the car while Clay remained, not sure where he had planned to go when he arrived in the lobby. The doors remained open until a middle-aged man wearing a suit and loosened tie entered the car and pressed the fifth floor button. As the doors began to close, the man asked Clay what floor he needed. Clay said five was good.

At the fifth floor, the man gestured for Clay to step off first. Clay didn't like the idea of turning his back on a stranger, but he felt he had no choice but to step off the car. Not sure whether to turn left or right, Clay chose left, and began walking down the hallway. He could hear footsteps behind him. The man from the elevator was following him. How could he have been such a fool as to let a button man get the drop on him?

Clay knew he had to make the first move. The man was probably gripping a gun in his pocket, trained on Clay's back. It was only a matter of seconds before that heater would be thrust against his spine and Clay would be told to shut up and keep on walking. There was no point worrying about how he had gotten himself into this mess. All that mattered was the play. And what was the play? Clay thought of a move. It was an old move, but still a good move. He would slow down and let the button man slip up on him, but at the last moment, Clay would move to the side and then backstep, grab him by the shoulders of his coat, pin his arms behind his back, and disarm him. It only worked if you were quick and smooth and didn't hesitate. You had to make a commitment to the move. If you didn't make a commitment to the move, the next thing you'd feel would be the police outlining your figure in chalk.

Clay was committed to the move, but just as he began to slow down, he heard the click of a lock. He looked over his shoulder to see the man in the suit with a key card in one hand. A moment later, Clay found himself alone in the hallway. Maybe this button man was playing the long game, in no hurry to make his move.

Clay doubled back to the elevator, smiling to himself. Now this was getting interesting. He loved a good cat and mouse game.

16

Waiting for the elevator, Clay checked his wrist watch. Did he need to be somewhere? Of course, the dry cleaning! Why did he keep forgetting about the dry cleaning? Clay jabbed both of the elevator call buttons until a car arrived. All the way down to the lobby, Clay cursed himself about forgetting the dry cleaning, cursed his dry cleaning for needing to be picked up. As soon as the doors broke open, Clay paced quickly through the hotel lobby, ignoring the night clerk, and onto the dark street beyond.

Clay now found himself on the sidewalk outside of the Hotel Windsor, out of breath and considering which way to turn. What was the address of that dry cleaning shop, anyway? Where was he standing, for that matter? According to the street signs, he was at the three-way intersection of Cherry, 17th, and the Ben Franklin Parkway. He could see City Hall a few blocks away and turned to walk in the opposite direction down Cherry Street, certain there were no dry cleaners to be found near City Hall. He walked past a bar and noticed through a plate glass window a baseball game playing on a television set. A couple of young men pushed open the doors to leave the joint and Clay asked them who won the game. It wasn't over yet, they told him. The Phillies and the Braves were tied at three apiece in the seventh.

Clay figured to have plenty of time to pick up his dry cleaning and still get home early enough to watch the end of the game. He liked to watch, or better yet listen, to baseball games from the first to the last pitch, but he knew plenty of people, especially the younger generation like his granddaughter, would rather skip to the end and avoid the first couple of hours.

"You're not a true fan," Clay told her more than once.

"I'm just not obsessed like you are."

Clay needed to get to the dry cleaners and back home if he was going to catch the end of the game. It was a big game. Was it a big game? It must be a big game. He was in a hurry, after all. Clay thought about the biggest game for the Three Musketeers when he was a kid. Well, it was a big game for Johnny, anyway. It was the final game of the season, the big one against the team from Providence that would determine the league championship. The last game of the year was all Johnny could talk about for days. Clay and Chuck tried to read detective stories in Clay's room, but it was hard to concentrate with Johnny talking about the game. They told him, as his best friends, his only friends, that the stupid game didn't matter, that nobody cared about the stupid game but him. It didn't help. Johnny was obsessed, and they just had to put up with him.

When the day of the big game arrived, it turned out that quite a few people in the town were also interested. Instead of a few parents and bored siblings, there were dozens of spectators who came to mill behind the backstop and benches to watch the game. It was a tight contest the entire way, and the longer it went, the more people gathered to watch. On the mound, Johnny struck out most of the Providence players, but the few balls that they managed to hit were botched by his fielders. Whatever runs his team gave up, however, Johnny got back at the plate, hitting a pair of homers. The game was tied in the bottom of the sixth, the final inning according to league rules, when Johnny had a chance to hit with two outs.

The outfielders backed up as far as they could. Johnny stared at the barrel of his bat, took a deep breath, stepped into the batter's box, tapped the plate twice, and looked out to the mound. Clay remembered how the pitcher looked scared. He held the ball, obviously not sure he wanted to risk offering a pitch. Finally, he dipped his glove to begin his windup.

"Time!" yelled the umpire.

The pitcher stopped his motion, and looked to left field. Walking in from the elementary school parking lot and heading for the infield was Johnny's dad.

"Get off the field!" The ump motioned towards the foul line while the spectators grumbled, but LeMaster ignored them. He proceeded in a straight line, cutting through the dirt infield until he reached home plate where Johnny stood with a bat on his shoulder.

"Come on, spud." LeMaster pulled the bat from Johnny and tossed it aside. "We have to get going."

"But, Pop, the game."

"It's just a game."

"It's almost over."

"It doesn't matter."

LeMaster grabbed Johnny above the elbow and pulled him away from the batter's box and began retracing his path across the infield toward the parking lot. Johnny tried briefly to pull himself free, but his father only tightened his grip. It was no use. He had to go. That's just the way it was, and nobody was going to interfere. Maybe LeMaster was just a fomenter of trouble and a likely atheist, but everyone in the crowd knew that a man, no matter who, had a right to do as he pleased with his own son. The game was held up as everybody watched Johnny step into his father's car and drive away.

Later, Clay and Chuck stopped by Johnny's house. His grandfather said Johnny had left with his Dad and he didn't think they would be coming back. A few days later, Chuck said he heard his parents talking about LeMaster and how he had gotten mixed up in some nasty business in Tower City, shot and killed some hired deputy, and was now running from the cops. It was big news in town for a couple of days, but pretty soon it was old news. Pretty soon everybody forgot about Johnny. Except for Clay and Chuck.

The three that had become one were now down to two, but otherwise nothing changed. Clay and Chuck continued to read their detective stories on the sly and waited impatiently until they grew up.

17

Just where in the world was he? Clay didn't recognize anything on the street. Ahead he saw a green shop sign that read "Coffee." Above it was another word, "Starbucks." Was he supposed to be meeting somebody? Was this the place? As he approached Starbucks Clay could see the faces of customers illuminated by the glow of laptops and those new Goddamn phones. Clay hated all of that electronic shit. There were still newspapers printed on paper but even they weren't like the old ones. The broadsheets weren't as broad as they used to be. He missed the old *Bulletin* and being able to hide behind it while keeping an eye on someone. When a kid made a sailor's hat from a sheet of the old *Bulletin*, it was big enough to satisfy the ego of an admiral. Not anymore.

Clay entered the Starbucks and sat at an open table and waited to be served. He watched someone place an order at the counter before remembering that at these new neon oases you had to do half the work. Oh, and you couldn't smoke. No fat newspaper, no ash tray, no waitress named Dottie to crack wise and freshen your joe. If this was progress, you could keep it. All he wanted was a cup of black coffee and a plain sinker but the boy at the counter said he had to pick a roast. Clover or Pike or the fucking "bold pick" of the day. Did he want a Short or a Grande or a Venti? And forget about a sinker. It was either a hand-forged doughnut or nothing at all. To pay for his order, Clay reached into his pants pocket for some change. A quarter back in the day would cover everything plus a tip, but not at this clip joint. He was lucky he found a twenty in his pocket.

Clay carried his cardboard cup of coffee and old fashioned glazed doughnut to an open table. There wasn't anything old fashioned about this trumped-up piece of pastry, and it didn't dunk worth a damn. It fell apart and the pieces just floated on the top of his cup of ridiculously hot coffee. You think Dottie would lug around a pot of this swill so hot you could weld with it? After Dottie made the round with a pot to top up the crowd, chatting with everybody as she went, you were lucky to get a splash of luke-warm wash. Perfect for dunking.

The hell with it all. Clay wasn't here for a mug of murk and a ringbolt. He was waiting for his man. He pushed the coffee and doughnut aside and gazed out the window, wondering if maybe the next guy he saw would be the one. Needing to take a piss, he didn't hesitate to leave his drink and food unattended. If it wasn't there when he got back, he'd spill no tears.

Even the bathroom at Starbucks was pretentious. All Clay wanted was a commode, a sink, a roll of sandpaper, and enough room to turn around, like the ones you used to find in the converted railroad-car diners he liked to frequent back in the day. The last time he was in one that size, it was a porta-john at the golf course. The smell of disinfectant was still fresh in mind.

While he pissed, Clay thought about that golf course porta-john. After some nagging from his wife, Clay's granddaughter, Steve had finally taken Clay along with him for a round of golf. The kid was anything but patient, rolling his eyes when Clay said he needed to use the toilet. Clay was hardly in the porta-john five seconds before Steve began rapping on the plastic shell with a pitching wedge. "You forget why you're in there, partner?" Once Clay emerged, Steve snatched him by the sleeve of his windbreaker and pulled him to the cart, telling him to just sit there and try not to tumble out and break a hip.

At the eighteenth green, Vivian was waiting for them. After Steve holed out, the three of them walked to the clubhouse, and she asked how the afternoon went.

"He had a swell time, honey." Steve's spikes clattered on the macadam path. "What's not to like? Fresh air. Birds singing. Right, partner?"

A few afternoons later, when Clay was supposed to go shopping for new pajamas with Vivian, she started to come down with a flu and asked Steve to fill in. Steve said he had an appointment with his attorney concerning some estate matters, and only after some prodding did he finally agree to bring Clay along and then take him shopping. Steve said next to nothing in the car, and Clay was going through a period in which his regrets in life were simply too overwhelming. More and more, Clay had retreated into a cocoon of senility to avoid the past. At one point during his day with Steve, Clay emerged momentarily to realize that he was sitting in the car by himself in a parking lot of a motel. The next thing Clay knew, Steve was slapping pajama bottoms across his belt to see if they fit.

Vivian wasn't too happy about the choice in pajamas. "Where'd you buy them?" she asked.

"Wal-Mart."

"You bought my grandfather PJs at Wal-Mart?"

"It was on the way home."

"I didn't ask you to buy him cheap pajamas. I wanted you to get him nice pajamas."

"If you wanted him to look like Hugh Hefner, you should have said so. Jesus, you'd think you'd be a little appreciative."

Vivian apologized. She was happy that Steve went out of his way to keep her grandfather company. She'd be even more thrilled if Steve would be able to find more chances to spend time with Clay.

"Doing what?"

"Anything. Just drive around the country. It doesn't matter."

Steve began to take Clay on long drives in the country, and soon he said he actually looked forward to their time together. Sometimes they went out two or three afternoons a week. Clay didn't care one way or the other, since fending off his memories in a car or on a couch made no difference. Vivian was pleased and eager to hear the details when they returned home.

"You enjoyed the cows, right partner?"

"What cows?"

"Trust me, Honey, he loved the cows."

"All I remember is the parking lot."

"Remember that Amishman in the buggy? He was kind of pissed when we buzzed him. You should have seen his horse rear up. It was funny as hell."

"It was a motel parking lot. I saw the sign when we pulled in. Dutch-something."

"We stopped for some bottles of water. Anyway, you should have seen that Amishman's face. It was priceless."

"I sat in the car for two hours."

"More like two minutes, but it probably felt that way. Still, we had a lot of fun. Hey, partner, I got an idea. Let's take in a Phillies game on Thursday."

"Who won the game?"

"They haven't played yet. It's a businessman's special. Game time twelve-thirty. We'll make a day of it."

Clay didn't recall the game. But he did remember the Wal-Mart. This time, Steve jammed a Phillies cap on his head to make sure it fit. He also remembered the parking lot of the Dutch-something Motel and Steve opening a mustard packet and dabbing some of the contents on the front of his shirt.

"Your grandfather has quite the appetite," Steve told Vivian at the end of the day. "What did you have, partner, three or four hot dogs?"

"I'm hungry."

"See, what I mean, honey? He could have had six more dogs and it wouldn't have been enough."

"I sat in the car all day."

"That's sure how it felt. God, I hate the Schuylkill Expressway."

"Who won the game?"

"The Phillies. Don't you remember? You high-fived everyone in the crowd."

"Did Del Ennis hit one?"

Clay washed his hands and returned to his table at Starbucks and was disappointed to find his coffee and doughnut still waiting for him. The faces of the same customers were illuminated by the same array of electronic nonsense. Clay sat down to wait and again look out the window. This didn't look like the Lower East Side. He was in New York, right? He was waiting in New York for the man who was going to give him the dope on why he had traveled cross-country. It had all seemed so urgent. Get your ass to the New York and somebody would fill you in. So here he was, waiting for his man.

While he was in the bathroom, somebody had dumped a Venti cup of overpriced coffee on the floor and one of the kids that worked behind the counter was wheeling out a bucket and mop to clean it up. It brought to mind a different mop in a bucket—the metal kind of bucket, not this yellow plastic whatever. It occupied the corner of the backroom office of his former client, Stoller. The guy had the dough to keep a nice office somewhere with a dish secretary, but instead he did business in what was really a janitor's closet and answered his own phone.

Stoller was simultaneously disgusted and glad to see Clay in the doorway. "I was wondering how you were spending my dough."

"I want to take a look at those blackmail notes."

Stoller picked at an apple fritter— definitely not hand-forged—laid out on a brown paper towel from the restroom, then licked his fingers, opened a desk drawer, and began to remove a manila folder with the corner of a light blue piece of paper showing, but stopped. "Wait. I already know who's behind it. Weren't we clear on what I want?" Stoller dropped the folder in the drawer and slammed it shut.

"The more I know, the better I can help you."

"Dirt. That's all I want from you. Are you getting anything on Pembroke or not?"

"He's got a girl on the side."

"Is that it? That's what fifty bucks a day buys these days?"

"You want a major blow-the-guy-out-of-the-water kind of scandal? That takes time."

"Meanwhile the meter keeps ticking. Neat trick."

"What do you know about the Hosiery Club of America?"

"What does that have to do with anything?"

"They make ladies' stockings. Sell 'em by mail. They're building a new plant in South Philly, only somebody's doing everything they can to stop it."

"You're losing me here."

"Have you ever heard of the company?"

"Is it important?"

"I think maybe it is. So what's the answer?"

"Okay, I'm a silent partner. I gave them that parcel of land for a piece of the business. It's a perfect location. The Jersey turnpike will swing that way and before you know it they'll build a bridge to connect South Philly. You could serve the whole Eastern Seaboard from there.

"Did Pembroke know about the deal?"

"Why should he?"

"You weren't cutting him out of this, were you?"

"Just a little side action. Like him and his girlfriends. So what?"

"Did you read about the suicide that took place down there?"

"Yeah, I sell newspapers."

"What if I told you that was no suicide but murder?"

"I'd be thrilled. We sell paperback mysteries, too."

"What if I told you your partner was on the scene?"

"You're saying Montgomery Pembroke gunned down a cop? The guy can't even take off his riding boots by himself."

"He was there before it happened. It seems somebody was putting pressure on Ellis to put pressure on his building inspector brother to shut down construction on the plant."

"What's that have to do with me? What's that have to do with Pembroke, for Christ's sake?"

"Well, Ellis seemed to think Pembroke was putting the squeeze on him to put the squeeze on his brother to shut down that plant. Pembroke must have had some dope on Ellis, some graft or something that wouldn't look good if it came out when the senators were in town."

"And that's exactly what I've been telling you. You fight fire with fire."

"So apparently Ellis thinks that Pembroke's upset that you double-crossed him on the HCA deal and maybe Pembroke was the one behind the threatening letters that he's been getting. His brother the inspector has received his share of threats, too. Not to mention HCA. Somebody's spending a lot of dough on postage in this town."

"Haven't you been listening to me? I know who's behind it. I didn't hire you to solve a puzzle that I already solved. I need material I can work with. Dirt. If you said Pembroke hired somebody to knock off a cop, that I can work with."

"He had nothing to do with it."

"Then find something that he did have something to do with!"

Stoller raised his hand, signaling Clay to be quiet. Soon a hint of perfume entered the room. Stoller smiled. "Hey, doll."

"Are you busy, darling?"

Clay turned in his chair to see Lynne standing in the doorway. She glanced at him and quickly looked down at her clutch, unclasping it like there was something she needed right away.

"So are we done here, Clay?"

"Am I interrupting something? Is this one of your new store managers?" Lynne pulled a cigarette case from her clutch

"Nothing like that."

"Is it a secret?"

"Actually, he's a private detective. And you always say I'm boring."

"A private eye. My god, darling, is there something the matter?"

"No, it's just store security stuff."

"Actually, your husband's a little disappointed about how little I have to offer," Clay said. "He thinks I'm wasting his money."

"Tell me, doll," Stoller said, "what brings you by?"

"It's that car again. It's in the shop. I told you not to buy it for me."

"How much this time?"

"Fifty should cover it." Stoller shifted in his chair to remove a roll of bills. "But make it a hundred. Just in case."

"How about sixty?"

"A hundred."

"Seventy-five."

"A hundred."

Stoller looked at Clay as he peeled off five twenties. "I spoil her."

Lynne stepped around the desk to pluck the money from Stoller's hand and peck his forehead.

"Isn't this a rare sight. Money leaving your grasp." Leaning against the doorway of the office was Pembroke, posing with one hand in a jacket pocket. "If only I had a Kodak. And how is the charming Mrs. Stoller?"

"I'm fine, Monty. How have you been? I haven't seen you in ages."

"It's been much too long. Have I told you, Stoller, I'm trying to persuade your beautiful wife to run away with me?" Pembroke turned his ivory smile on Clay and extended his hand. "I don't believe I've had the pleasure."

"This is Clay White," Stoller said.

"Be careful, Monty, he's a private detective." Lynne plucked a cigarette from her case and Pembroke was quick to fish a jeweled lighter from his pocket. "I think he's found us out."

"Oh dear. This is awkward." Pembroke stepped forward to offer a flame to Lynne's cigarette.

"I think one of my managers has got a case of light fingers," Stoller said. "Don't you have a car to deal with, doll?"

Stoller asked Clay if he minded dropping off his wife at the garage. A few seconds later, Clay and Lynne were walking out of Stoller's office together. Neither spoke as they passed through the store and rattled a bell, ting-a-ling-a-ling, at the front door on the way to his car.

18

The kid at Starbucks wheeled away the mop and bucket, leaving Clay to wonder again when his man would show. Clay wasn't sure who to look for, but it didn't matter as long as he carried the matching box top. Clay was now afraid that he had lost his half. He patted his windbreaker pockets and felt something stiff and flat in one of them. He reached inside and removed a small paper envelop with a hotel keycard inside. Clay turned over the envelop. On it was written "#809." The name and address of a hotel was also printed on the envelope. Was that where the meeting was to take place? Not in this dump but a hotel room? The guy was probably waiting for him right now.

Clay raised a hand to catch the attention of the green-aproned kid who had just finished mopping the floor. "I need my check."

"What?"

"My check, Einstein."

"Dude, you already paid."

A moment later, Clay was on the street, walking furiously and wondering why he was walking furiously and to where. He was obviously in a hurry, but why? Was he being chased? He glanced over his shoulder and saw no one. Maybe he was the one doing the chasing. Ahead, Clay spotted a man walking slowly, head bowed. Clay was already winded but he was still able to catch up to the man and lay a hand on his shoulder to turn him around. The guy was sobbing. Why was Clay following a crying man?

"I'm okay," the man said. "It's just hard to accept he's gone."

"Who's gone?"

"My boy. He's dead."

"Sorry. I thought you were somebody else."

Clay turned to walk in a different direction and leave the man to his grief. Some kid was dead. That was hardly front page news. Hell, some kids were dead to their parents even before they died. Take Clay for example. He and Chuck grew up and muddled their way through high school. Maybe Clay had turned into the P.K. that proved an embarrassment to his father on earth as well as in Heaven, but he was still expected to enroll in the Bible college of his parents' choice. He didn't bother telling them that he didn't want to go, but he really didn't know what else he wanted to do after high school. There was a good chance he'd end up at Bible college simply because it was the easy thing to do. Just like staying friends with Chuck.

Chuck grew taller and lost the fat. His lazy eye also improved, and if he hadn't been such an annoying jerk for so many years, the girls might have taken more notice of him. He still wanted to become a private detective. Or maybe he would join the Foreign Legion. In any case, he wanted to escape this town to kill people and fornicate for a living.

Then came that day that changed their lives, and a lot of people's lives. One of those days that became one of those stories of where you were and what you were doing. Clay and Chuck were drinking Nehi sodas, sitting on the bench in front of the town's lone filling station on an unusually mild December afternoon. People waiting for the Lancaster bus usually sat on this bench provided by the Red Rose Transit Company, but it being a Sunday, no bus was scheduled that day. Clay tried to listen to "Chattanooga Choo Choo" on the crackling radio playing in the garage rather than to Chuck, who had been debating for several minutes the best way to mate with sheep. The song suddenly stopped but the crackling continued. A few seconds later, an announcer broke in to report that according to the Associated Press, Japanese forces had just bombed the U.S. Naval base at Pearl Harbor in the Hawaiian Islands. The attendant pumping gas stood with nozzle in hand, and the driver of the car leaned out his window, craning to hear the radio. Clay recognized that this was major news, that America was at war. He also knew that he and Chuck, both on the verge of turning 18, were ripe for the military draft that had been instituted the previous year.

At first, Chuck ignored the radio and the nervous chatter of the people who were beginning to gather around the garage radio. Soon, even he was listening to the reports of other air raids in the South Pacific. After a few minutes, Chuck swallowed the last of his Nehi. "Come on, Clay. Let's go. This is boring."

Instead of wasting the rest of the afternoon with Chuck or listening to the news at the filling station, Clay returned home to find his parents in the living room knelt in prayer. The news of Pearl Harbor was especially troubling for the Reverend White because he had spent the past twenty years a determined isolationist, and during the previous decade he had been a staunch opponent of President Roosevelt. In a matter of moments all of that had changed. Clay heard his father pray that the Lord grant strength and wisdom to FDR, the man He had appointed to lead the country during its upcoming trials.

Unnoticed by his parents, Clay slipped into the kitchen and cut a wedge of deep-dish apple pie. He removed a bottle of milk from the ice box and sat at the breakfast table when his father entered.

"It's war for certain." The Rev stood hands in sweater pockets in the doorway.

Clay sat at the table, poured a glass of milk, took up his fork.

"You have heard the news, I trust," his father said.

"I'm eating."

Clay's mother then appeared in the doorway. The Rev reached up to put his arm around her waist, perhaps for the first time since the last world war.

Clay stared at his pie and ate. He only looked up at his parents when he paused for a drink of milk. "I know. The Japs bombed Pearl Harbor. Can I eat in peace now?"

"Your mother and I," said The Rev, "were wondering how many 17-year-old boys such as yourself were at this very moment begging their parents to allow them to join up early."

"Join up?"

"Military service, Clay. The Army. The Navy."

"I'm still in high school."

"We would have refused the request, of course… until graduation. We were just speculating about how many young men were actually eager to enlist. But perhaps we're interrupting your snack."

Clay finished off his pie while his parents continued to watch from the doorway. "You don't think I'm taking this seriously enough, do you?"

"Not especially."

"Actually I have been giving it some thought and have come to a decision."

"Really?"

"I can't wait to hear," said his mother.

"I'm becoming a conscientious objector."

"You're what?" The Rev's face began to ripen with rage.

"You've always taught me to follow my conscience, and I believe killing is wrong no matter what the reason. 'Thou shalt not kill.' Period. End of subject."

"You leave the Bible out of this, young man!"

"My heart is set. I will not fight. I will not help others fight. If I have to, I'll go to jail, but I will not fight."

Clay's mother pushed herself away from the Reverend White, and without a word stepped over to Clay and cuffed him on the side of the head. "You won't fight? My son won't fight." She struck him again. "You're going to humiliate me in this community because you're too afraid to fight?"

Clay did not raise his hands to ward off the blows, just lowered his head slightly. She hit him again before The Rev clutched her by the shoulders and pulled her away. "My dear, please."

"You shut up!" Clay's mother now turned on The Rev, striking his chest with a hammer fist. "I suffered through two miscarriages and was worried sick the entire time I carried him. And for what? To be laughed at behind my back? How dare you, Clay! How dare both of you treat me like this. As if I don't matter. As if I'm trash. The both of you are weak. I'm tired of sacrificing my life for you two…disappointments."

"You're just upset." The Rev tried to hug his wife, but she pushed him away and began backing out of the kitchen. "Go on, Clay. Do what you want. We'll see what happens once your friends go into the service while you try to shirk your responsibility. We'll see how conscientious you are then."

"I won't kill. I can't."

"That's where you're wrong. At heart, we're all killers. Every last one of us. Do you know what motherhood is, Clay? It's slowly being murdered by your children."

Clay's mother turned her back on husband and son and carried her anger upstairs. Stunned, father and son looked at one other. Finally the Reverend White spoke up. "We need to do something nice for her."

19

Clay crossed the street, leaving behind the Starbucks on the corner, and a man grieving over his son. It must have been a war to blame. What war, Clay couldn't say. There was always a war somewhere, right? There were always a lot of fathers and mothers who grieved over children lost in war. Clay supposed that the Reverend and Mrs. White had lost a child to war in their own way, too.

As his 18th birthday approached in the spring of 1942, Clay became secretly obsessed with the war news. While his parents read the newspaper and listened to the radio in the living room to keep up with the latest developments in Europe and the Pacific campaign, Clay appeared indifferent to world events. Late at night, however, he rescued the newspaper from the trash, smuggled it upstairs to his room, and read the war news on the sly. He sat on the floor by the side of his bed hidden from the door, reading the paper while the nightstand radio offered the news on the quiet. London calling. Whispering.

After Pearl Harbor, the Reverend and Mrs. White said nothing more about Clay's military service. They said little to each other, for that matter. The rectory endured its own multi-front war. His mother continued to put on her face for the neighbors and the flock, and at home she continued to cook and keep house, but she only spoke when necessary. At the dinner table, The Rev continued to bless the food but kept the commentary to a minimum.

While many young men in the area had already enlisted in the military, and others received their draft notices or reached the age when they were required to register for the draft, the Amish community found itself impacted as well. There had always been an uneasy relationship between the sect and its worldly neighbors, but now the war brought their differences into greater relief. Like the Quakers and Jehovah's Witnesses, the Amish practiced a peaceful religion and were adamantly opposed to military service. For them, the only question was how far to accommodate the government. Were you willing to serve as a noncombatant or perhaps a medic, or would you prefer going to prison rather than participate in even the most minor role in the war effort? Unlike the first World War, when those who refused to cooperate with the government were locked up and all too often abused by patriotic guards and inmates, there was a new middle ground, one that attracted Clay's attention: Civilian Public Service, CPS, a work camp program for conscientious objectors, CO's.

The vast majority of CO's were white, and the authorities felt no need to round them up for internment in concentration camps like those of

Japanese descent. Instead, approved CO's were allowed to intern themselves in unguarded work camps, digging sewers and completing other public works projects in poor communities, or toiling in the nation's great forests that needed tending. Of course, the CO's were not to be paid for their labor. This was punishment, after all, although officially there was no punishment for following your conscience. In any event, a work camp for likeminded people was better than serving time in prison. What was a little yard work compared to being sodomized with a broom handle?

While he privately followed the war news, Clay publicly laid the groundwork for becoming a conscientious objector. He took church more seriously, forcing Chuck to sit closer to the front of the congregation. Clay could even be counted on now to offer prayer topics when The Rev made his weekly appeal to the flock.

Chuck accused Clay of putting on an act, but accepted Clay's explanation that he was trying to get on the good side of his folks in order to borrow the family car. Chuck had never been one to discuss the news, and initially a world war proved no different, but as he too approached his 18th birthday, Chuck realized that the war was going to impact his life as well, and he now began to follow the war news with a bit more interest. He began to see the war as his ticket out of a small town, as a way to fulfill all of his long-held desires. He became eager to join the Army after high school graduation. He pestered Clay about joining up with him until Clay finally admitted he was going to declare as a conscientious objector. Chuck said he didn't believe him.

As his 18th birthday approached, Clay wrote to the draft board, requesting the necessary forms to file for CO designation. After a few days, he began to check the mail box, hoping to intercept the draft board's reply without his parents' interference. Finally a fat envelop from Selective Service arrived. He stuffed it down the leg of his trousers and smuggled it inside the rectory. He waited until late at night, sitting on the floor of his bedroom with the war news playing lightly in the background, to finally open the envelop.

The application for CO status was broken into three series of questions. In Series I, the applicant was offered a pair of choices. A: Was he willing to serve in the military in a non-combatant capacity? Or B: Was he so opposed to war that he would only perform alternative service? There was an additional, however unstated, option C: prison time. Series II consisted of two essay questions intended to determine the sincerity of the answers to Series I. What were the nature of the applicant's beliefs that prohibited him from killing, and how were they grounded in religion? How, when, and from whom or what source did he receive his religious training? How did those beliefs restrict him from ministering to battlefield wounded or serving in some other non-combatant role? Moreover, had the applicant ever expressed his views publicly or privately, orally or written? Finally, Series III provided space for the listing of references, the names and addresses of people who could back up the assertions made in Series II.

Clay immediately lost heart. The application seemed too onerous. He stashed the paperwork between his box spring and mattress, where it remained untouched for three days before he again considered it. He then took up pen and paper and slowly began to work his way through the questions. After a week of writing and editing, he posted his application to the Draft Board, and then went home and straight to bed. He must have caught a summer cold, he said.

On his 18th birthday, Chuck took the bus to Lancaster and enlisted in the Army. A few days later, he and Clay sat together on the bench outside the filling station waiting for the Lancaster bus that would take Chuck to basic training. Clay missed Chuck almost as soon as the bus pulled away. He found himself genuinely excited when a letter from Chuck arrived a few days later. Although neither one had liked to write in school, they now corresponded regularly. Chuck reported that his remaining baby fat had melted away and that he was starting to look forward to the long runs in heavy boots, the pushups, the sit ups, all of it. He also turned out to be a good shot, this from a kid who once had a lazy eye. He became his platoon's champion pugil stick fighter. On his first leave, Chuck got drunk for the first time in his life. On his second leave, he cast off his virginity. He wrote that he couldn't wait to ship out. That's when the real fun would begin. Clay didn't know what he was missing, the biggest carnival the world had ever seen. Thank God for the war.

After weeks of waiting, Clay finally received his reply from the Draft Board. The envelope had already been peeled open. An enclosed letter informed him that after careful consideration, his application had been denied.

That night at dinner, Clay's mother was in an especially good mood. "Father, did Clay tell you he received a letter from the Draft Board?"

"What? What's that?"

"Do you have anything to tell your father, Clay?"

Clay laid down his knife and fork, and dabbed his lips with a napkin.

"My application for conscientious objector status was turned down."

"That foolishness is settled then," his father said.

"Actually, I plan to appeal the decision to the state board."

"I think not," said his mother.

"It's all part of the process. Just to make sure you're serious. They want to hear from witnesses."

"I think we need to pray about this," replied the Reverend White.

"I have prayed about it."

"Maybe we need to pray some more."

"I have prayed some more. I believe this is God's will."

"Perhaps we should pray about it together."

"This has gone well beyond prayer!" Clay's mother's mood had taken a quick turn for the worse. She snapped at The Rev. "Prayer? Is that all you have to offer?"

"Mother, please—"

"You tricked me into marrying you! If you were the real go-getter you claimed to be, we would have left for a bigger church years ago. You know what a real go-getter does? He preaches on the radio. He holds revivals at hockey rinks. He creates mailing lists and people send him money. But not you. You read your books and write your sermons and pretend you're a theologian, like you're some kind of John Wesley. You know what you really are? You're just a little man with an oversized opinion of himself."

Clay's mother crumpled her napkin and dropped it on the table as she rose and left the room. Clay looked at his father, who appeared stunned. And old. The Reverend White took a sip of water, returned to eating his meal while keeping his eyes on his plate. "As I was saying, we need to pray on this matter."

"What about Mom?"

"Don't change the subject."

"You're the one trying to change the subject. I think Mom needs help."

"You can help her, Clay, by living up to your patriotic duty."

"She's having a nervous breakdown."

"Over your conduct!"

"No. It's you. It's always been you. Everything is about you. About living up to your image in the community."

"That's enough!"

"Well, I don't care about your image. I'm going to appeal. And if I have to, I'll go to prison to uphold my beliefs."

"Beliefs? What beliefs?"

"You'll see." Now Clay was the one to leave the room abruptly.

20

Clay was lost in his thoughts on the streets of Philadelphia, but he needed to focus. He was on his way to an urgent meeting. What he needed to know was where the meeting was to be held and with whom. He approached the bright lights of a WaWa convenience store. Was this one of Stoller's stores? Clay watched a man and a woman exit the WaWa and leave in a car parked in front. He remembered the time he and Lynne left together from Stoller's store, right after he learned she was the guy's wife. Clay had driven for a full block before asking Lynne for the location of the garage that was supposed to be working on her car.

"The car's fine. I just needed some more cash. How's that for honesty?" She then directed him to where she had parked the car on the street.

While they waited at a stoplight, Clay asked, "You been married long?"

"One year, five months, seven days, three hours, ten minutes."

"You're a lady who like to keep score."

"I make a notch on the wall every morning I wake up."

"Isn't that how most people count down the days?"

"I'm unusual that way." Lynne pulled a compact from her clutch and began to fix her face. "I suppose I underestimated you. You must be having a good laugh at my expense. Speaking of which, how much do you plan to soak me for?"

Clay didn't answer, just made a turn.

"I'm sorry, was that rude? I've never been blackmailed before."

"I didn't even know you were married to the man until five minutes ago."

"Then why were you following me?"

"I was following Monty. You were following him. So I started to follow you instead."

"Why?"

"I'm curious…about a lot of things."

"So what do you want, I mean really want?"

"Answers."

"Answers? To questions? I thought you were the action type. You just come out guns blazing and sort it all out later."

"I bet you really go for the action type. The type that just does what you want without thinking it through. Like Nicky."

"Nicky?"

"He likes to come out guns blazing."

"Oh, that Nicky."

"How'd you meet him?"

"Probably some social event. Oh, I remember. It was a dinner at the art museum to raise money. I had to

162

drag my husband there, and to tell you the truth, I hate art. I just like to be seen with it. They had a charity auction and as you can imagine my husband didn't see fit to make even a courtesy bid. I suppose I was a little annoyed and showed it. Nicky noticed and began to bid on something while looking my way."

"Trying to impress you?"

"He did impress me. Tall, rich, spoiled. Just the way I like them."

"Are you sure that wasn't Monty?"

"Perhaps it was. Sometimes it's not easy for the spider to keep track of all the flies in her web."

"All those flies and you settled for Stoller. But maybe he was just your ticket to the Main Line. A guy with enough money to get you in the door. Then you could trade up."

"You really think you have me pegged."

"Monty was your trade up. Only Monty wasn't looking for a new hostess. He already has the perfect wife to arrange that dinner party with Bunny Lippincott. He doesn't have the time to teach some lemon tart the difference between a pitch fork and a salad fork. All Monty wanted was what Monty wanted. And when you wanted more, he wanted less."

"Funny how that works."

"So now maybe you're wishing the worst for him."

"My husband. Monty. Perhaps Nicky. Perhaps you. What's a spider to do? There's my car."

Clay eased his sedan to a stop and without the investment of another word, Lynne stepped out.

Clay drove to Shibe Park to watch the Athletics play the Red Sox, to think about baseball for a while and nothing else. There was no problem finding a ticket, just someone to sell it to him. The A's were lucky if 2,000 people were in the park. The team once owned the town, and they still owned the ball park. The Phillies were the renters. It was a way to kill some time at least. Clay returned to his office and found a business card tucked under the door. It was from Pembroke. On the back was a note asking Clay to stop by his estate the following afternoon.

Clay sat at his desk, tapping Pembroke's card on the blotter when he heard a tapping on the frosted glass of the front door to the outer office. The caller was the peroxide blonde. Phyllis Ryan. Clay recognized the outfit she was wearing as one of the purchases from the shopping trip the other day: a bankers grey chemise with a stole draped over her shoulders. She clutched a hankie in her gloved hands and in a shaky voice asked if she could come in. Clay offered her one of the chairs in his office and sat behind the desk, watching her take a seat and dab at the corner of her eyes, heavy with mascara. A lot of women were going for the "doe-eyed" effect that year, but it only took a tear or two to make a disaster of it all.

"Please forgive me. I'm a bit upset."

"Would a drink help? There's a bottle in the desk."

"That's kind, but no. It's about Lynne. She's always been a little foolish, but I'm afraid this time she's gone too far."

Phyllis opened her purse and removed a piece of light blue paper, unfolded it, and held it out to Clay: TO KEEP THE KID'S HUSBAND DUMB: $10,000. 2 DAYS. INSTRUCTIONS TO FOLLOW.

"Keep her husband dumb about what?" Clay returned the paper.

"I think we both know the answer to that one."

"For the record then."

"Her affair. Her affair with her husband's partner."

"When did you receive this?"

"This morning. In the mail."

"So you know all about Lynne and Pembroke?"

"She tells me everything. We're a lot closer than a regular mother and daughter."

"Maybe because you're not. How is that exactly?"

Phyllis gave Clay the complete sob story. How she became best friends with Lynne's mom, Gertie, who had run away from home at sixteen. They were both just a couple of kids trying to find costume work in Hollywood. They were as close as sisters. When Gertie got in trouble and had a baby after some rat ran out on her, Phyllis helped to raise Lynne.

"But Gertie never learned her lesson and got herself in trouble again, only this time it didn't go so well," Phyllis said.

Her friend died with a stillborn baby. Phyllis had been taking care of Lynne. So what was she supposed to do now? She didn't know how to reach Gertie's family, and even if she did, Gertie's family didn't sound like a good place for little Lynne.

"I couldn't let her be taken away to some orphanage or wherever, so I decided to raise Lynne as my own daughter. And it's not like anybody was looking for the baby. Gertie was a hospital charity case."

To support them, Phyllis was able to find sewing work at Warner Brothers, but she had to give up on her dreams of becoming a costumer designer. Eventually she became a wardrobe assistant, but it was hardly the glamorous life she had always imagined. Lynne in the meantime grew to become a pretty little girl, who stood out because of the clothes Phyllis made for her from costume shop remnants. Shirley Temple was all the rage at the time, and Phyllis didn't see any reason why Lynne couldn't pull the same stunt. Phyllis had met enough people to get Lynne a screen test. Fox had Shirley Temple and all the other studios were desperate to find the next child star. Lynne looked good on screen, good enough to at least land a couple of bit roles over the next few years. The highlight of her acting career was kicking Cary Grant in the shins. It wasn't much of a resume but more than enough to make her feel special.

"I didn't help any. I admit it. I became a bit of a stage mother. I guess I will have that drink." While Clay found a clean enough glass and poured two fingers, Phyllis said that Lynne grew up to become a beautiful young woman but despite her looks she still couldn't act. At least on camera. Instead of work, she just found trouble. There were some drugs. Then there was that producer who said he wanted to cast her in one of his pet projects, namely himself. Phyllis had met and married Ryan by this time. He was a studio fixer, a guy who kept tabs on the stars and cleaned up their messes.

"Then the war came, Paul got drafted and lost an arm," Phyllis said. "When he came back, the studios didn't need him, and a stab at being a private eye didn't pan out either."

"That's when you moved to Philly so he could take the job at HCA."

"We needed to leave, anyway."

"You mean, you needed to get Lynne out of town."

"That was part of it."

"How'd she meet Stoller?"

"They met. That's all that matters."

"I guess they had a lot in common. Mutual love of his bank account."

"It's easy to be critical, Mr. White. But why shouldn't she find a rich husband? It's every woman's right to seek and find security. God knows few of us ever do."

"Fine, if that's what she wanted. But you know that's not your girl. She wants to hang with the hot set, and in Philly that means the Main Line crowd. In particular, Monty Pembroke. A guy oozing with all the sophistication and charm that Stoller lacks in great abundance."

"She's tried to keep it a secret from me. But I knew. I also knew that despite what he might say, Monty doesn't love her. And he certainly isn't going to leave his wife over her. Lynne's just a diversion."

"Try telling that to the diversion."

"I think she knows it's a mistake. She knows she has a good thing in Stoller."

"He makes her feel secure. I heard."

"I don't want her to ruin her marriage. To make a mistake she'll regret for the rest of her life."

"Yeah, it would be a terrible thing to see all of Stoller's dough go to waste. Whoever sent you that note seems to think it's worth ten large to keep the guy in the dark at least until …"

"Until what?"

"They read the will."

"Don't even suggest such a thing as a joke."

"Little Miss is the one doing all the suggesting."

"She says things she doesn't mean."

"She means things she doesn't say."

"She's young, she can be foolish, but she's a good girl at heart."

"Okay, she's a swell kid. The kind they stopped minting ages ago. So why are you coming to me?"

"I don't have the money. Maybe I can raise a thousand. In a few months I can give you another thousand or so. I have a little something on me." Phyllis began to open her purse.

"You think I'm the one trying to shake you down? I must have a worse reputation than I figured."

"If it's not you…" Phyllis stopped short on opening the purse. Instead, she slowly reached across the desk for the blackmail note but paused before she reached it. "Perhaps you could find out who it is and make it stop? Would a hundred dollars be enough for a retainer?"

"Keep your dough," Clay said. "I'll do what I can."

21

Clay inspected the aisles of the WaWa. It certainly had a lot more to offer than Stoller's old store with its meager shelves of canned and packaged goods and cold cases of milk and beverages. The WaWa had carafes of coffee and hot sandwiches for sale and a ridiculous variety of cold drinks and snacks. Half the walls were lined with refrigerated cases, filled top to bottom with soft drinks, iced teas, energy drinks, and bottled waters. People bought water these days? It was crazy. They didn't just buy water, they bought it and didn't drink it. When Clay had taken those rides in the country with Steve, the kid always picked up plastic bottles of water, took a sip or two and just left the bottle sitting in the cup holder. If Clay didn't finish his bottle of water, he made sure to take it with him when he got out of the car.

After one of their outings, Clay and Steve were met by Vivian and young Tom Pembroke. Clay clutched his bottle of water in both hands, determined not to forget about it.

"You must be thirsty," Tom said. "I know spending time with Steve makes me want a drink."

Steve smiled behind a pair of mirrored sunglasses. "You can't say I don't keep him hydrated."

"You guys are spending a lot of time together. Could it be love?"

"I'm proud of him." Vivian squeezed her husband's arm.

"But seriously, Clay, did you have a good time? What did you do today?"

"Sat in the car. In a parking lot."

"That Goddamn expressway," Steve said. "They really need to add another lane or two."

"Maybe I could take Clay out some afternoon," Tom said. "Maybe get the old private eye to tell me some of his old war stories."

"You should," Vivian said. "I think he would love it."

"He can be a handful," Steve said. "Just warning you."

"Hey, I'm game for anything." Tom answered.

The next day, Tom showed up to take Clay for a drive, but he didn't ask him about the old days. Instead, he asked a lot of questions about the present, about which direction he and Steve took when they went out for their afternoon drives.

"Any of this look familiar, Clay? Do you remember any motels?"

"Motel?"

"You remember any names?"

"Dutch-something. There was a bird on the sign."

"What kind of bird?"

"A bird with two heads."

They traveled west on Route 30, Tom occasionally stopping at convenience stores to ask directions. Finally, he spotted the double-headed bird, a Pennsylvania Dutch hex sign. They pulled into the parking lot of the Dutch Treat Motel, and while Clay waited in the car, Tom paid a visit to the office. He emerged a few minutes later. Smiling.

When Clay and Tom returned from their afternoon drive, they were met by Vivian as expected, but she wasn't alone. She was joined by Steve.

"I hope he wasn't too much for you," Steve said. "His imagination can run a little wild."

"He seemed pretty lucid to me. I think getting out is good for him."

"Absolutely." Vivian placed her hand behind Clay's back and began to rub it in circles.

"I'll take him tomorrow," Steve said.

"Clay and I already made plans. Right, sir?"

"Come on, Tom. It's my turn."

"We don't want to disappoint him."

"Grandpa, they're fighting over you!" Vivian was pleased, but finally she had to step in and decide that it was Steve's turn to spend the afternoon with Clay.

"But I have an idea," she said. "One of these days, you can both take him out. Maybe he could ride along in a cart while you play golf."

The following afternoon, Steve and Clay went for another one of their drives. Often Steve listened to music when they went out. Sometimes Clay said the music was too loud and asked Steve to turn it down. Usually Steve ignored him. Other times he smiled and said, "I can't hear you! The music's too loud!" But he never turned it down. On this day, however, there was no music.

"Do you know who won the game?" Clay asked.

"Last night? The Mets. They shut 'em out. Do you remember which direction you took, which highway?"

"We went to see the birds."

"Tom took you bird watching? What, with binoculars?"

"The birds are huge."

"What are you saying, Clay? He took you to an ostrich farm?"

"They look more like pigeons."

"Did you go into the city to feed pigeons?"

"Dutch treat."

"He made you pay?"

"The birds on the sign. Dutch treat."

"Oh shit, you took him to the Dutch Treat Motel? What the fuck were you thinking?"

"I hate those birds."

"Did you just drive by, or did you stop in?"

Clay looked at the scenery as it slipped past.

"Clay, did Steve go into the motel?"

"He said he needed to use the bathroom."

"I bet he did."

Clay fell asleep in the car. When he woke up he saw the birds. Steve's car was parked under the large Dutch Treat Motel sign. A minute later, Clay saw Steve leaving the office and walking toward the car. He slipped in and sat behind the steering wheel, gripping it for several seconds while glaring straight ahead.

"I know it's not your fault." Slowly Steve removed his right hand from the wheel, pulled it back, and then snapped his arm through the air, striking Clay on the side of the jaw and forcing his head against the headrest.

They listened to music all the way home. Full blast.

The next morning, Clay's caregiver told him that his granddaughter had come to visit. From where he was sitting in the sunroom, Clay could see Vivian place a suitcase on the floor by the stairs. She could see he saw the suitcase. After kissing him on the forehead, she asked if he wouldn't mind having her stay with him for a while.

"Running from trouble?" Clay was having one of his more talkative, if not cogent, days in a while.

"Maybe I just want to spend more time with you."

"I can't help you unless you give me the straight dope."

"That's my grandpa. Always on the case."

That night Steve showed up. He didn't stay long. The following day, Tom Pembroke made an appearance. Clay was eating his breakfast in the sunroom when he saw Pembroke rapping on the glass and letting himself in.

"Hi there, Mr. White. How are the prunes this morning?"

"Is this a shakedown? Better have brought some more muscle with you."

"You're a trip. Is Vivian awake?"

"I don't eat prunes, you piece of shit!"

"You wouldn't happen to know if she hired a lawyer?"

Clay's caregiver told Vivian that Tom was downstairs. Vivian didn't look especially pleased to see him, and turned away when he tried to give her a peck on the cheek.

"I talked to Steve last night," she said. "Now he sends you to plead his case."

"He didn't send me, Viv. I just stopped by on my own."

"To see my grandfather? Everybody loves to spend time with grandpa all of a sudden."

"I just want you to know that if there's anything you need, I'm here. Steve's my best friend and everything, but right is right."

"Thanks."

"You guys have a good thing going. It's tough when you lose trust in someone you love. Maybe it's something you'll never get back. Who's to say that if you forgive him he won't do it again?"

"That's reassuring."

"Sorry, that didn't come out right. I'm just saying don't give up too soon. That's all I'm trying to say."

"Thanks, I really do appreciate that."

Tom rose from his chair and patted Clay on the back. "And it was good seeing you again, sir. Hey, you feel like going to the movies tonight?"

Vivian thought that was a wonderful idea and accepted on Clay's behalf.

Steve also came by the house that night. He stayed a little longer than his previous visit. He even stepped into the living room to give his best to Clay watching *The Big Sleep* on Channel 17 while he waited for Tom to pick him up for their movie date.

"You again," Clay said. "Think you can rough me up and I'll spill the beans?"

"Are you sure you should let him watch these kinds of movies?"

"He likes his detective stories," Vivian said. "What's the harm?"

A few minutes after Steve left, Tom arrived. He drove Clay to a suburban multiplex. After he parked the car and turned off the engine, Clay unbuckled his seat belt and reached for the door handle, but Tom stopped him, saying he had to do something first. He leaned over to the glove box, removed a leather pouch, and from it pulled out a small mirror, razor blade, a short section of straw, and a mint tin. He tapped some white powder onto the mirror.

"What's that?" Clay asked.

"Doctor's orders." Tom prepared two lines of powder on the mirror and drew them up each nostril. "Hey, you got any money? I forgot my ATM card."

Tom pulled Clay's wallet from his jacket and inside the theater drew on it to buy the tickets and load up on popcorn, candy, and a bucket of soda. They then found their screen. Tom admitted they were going to see a chick flick, but he had seen everything else already.

From the opening moment of the film, Tom began laughing and quickly received some disapproving looks, followed later by clicking tongues. Finally, some assistant manager with a flashlight walked down the aisle and asked Tom to tone it down.

"I'm sorry, but it's funny."

"It's an uplifting story about cancer, sir. It's not supposed to be funny."

Tom promised to be respectful and was quiet for a minute or two before he exploded with laughter when a bald woman on a blind date vomited in some bushes. They were now politely asked by the assistant manager to leave. Tom got his—Clay's—money back. He said it was just as well. There was a party he knew about.

At the party, Tom parked Clay in the corner with a plastic cup of beer. A few minutes later he brought over some friends.

"You enjoying the movie, Clay?"

"What movie?"

"Having fun?"

"Huh?"

"He's gonna tell his granddaughter."

"Tell her what? Tomorrow he won't remember if he was at the movies or on the moon. And she'll be so pleased I took her gramps out."

"You're sick, dude."

"He's having fun. You're having fun, right, Clay?"

Clay sat on the couch for the next three hours. Tom then drove him home, stuffed his wallet back into his jacket pocket, and walked him to the door. Vivian couldn't have been happier that her grandfather had enjoyed such a wonderful evening, going to the movies and then pizza afterwards.

"The pleasure was all mine," Tom said. "Maybe next time I could take you to the movies."

She smiled. "I'll have to think about that."

Vivian did not go to the movies with Tom. Steve began showing up at Clay's house every day, and he and Vivian spent longer periods of time with each other. A week after Vivian came to stay with Clay, she showed up with her suitcase to tell Clay that she was going home. She had been away long enough, but she'd be back to visit soon, and maybe one of the boys would come to take him out again soon.

One morning, while Clay was eating his toast, Steve appeared. "Saddle up, partner. Me and Tom are taking you golfing."

Forty minutes later, they met Pembroke outside the pro shop.

"How's Vivian?" Pembroke was sitting on a bench tightening the laces of his spikes.

"It's all good." Steve was smoking a cigar, inspecting it rather than looking at Tom.

"Glad to hear it."

"In time, I think it will make us stronger."

A pair of electric Club Cars waited for them near the first tee. While the foursome ahead of them walked after their opening drives, Steve and Tom stretched and loosened up.

"You need to find someone steady in your life, Tom."

"I'm doing okay."

"No, seriously. You need a little stability in your life. Of course, what you really need is a steady income."

"I'm fine. Maybe not like you. But I'm doing okay."

"Doing okay doing what?"

"You know I don't like to talk about business."

"Small-time dealing? Come on, where's that going to get you, other than five to ten?"

"That was just a lark. I don't do that anymore."

"So what do you do for money?"

"I have irons in the fire."

"Really?"

"Yeah, really. Enough to say I can take you for a hundred bucks a hole. Unless that's too rich for your blood."

"Hundred bucks a hole? Hell, I bet you don't have a hundred bucks to your name. What do you think, Clay? Is your boy good for it when I wax his ass?"

"I don't have a boy."

"Sure. Tom's your boy. Didn't you know, you're his role model, you and that hardboiled life you led back in the day."

"Are you taking the bet, or are you going to pussy out?"

"You're on." Steve disposed of the cigar and stepped to the tee for his first drive. Clay watched from his seat in the golf cart.

All in all, it was a pleasant morning. The sun was out and the air was crisp. The birds were singing. The bees were busy. One of them was especially industrious.

22

Clay looked at his reflection in a silver globe that housed a security camera in the WaWa store. Everything was self-serve these days. When Clay was growing up, grocery stores still had clerks that waited on you and filled your orders. They wore white aprons and were obsequious, the way God intended. At least, that was the way The Rev saw it. He used to say at the dinner table that he had no use for those Piggly Wiggly stores that allowed customers to pick items off the shelves by themselves. It was a slippery slope, The Rev had warned. Self-service today, eternal damnation tomorrow. It was the kind of argument that sometimes made its way into a sermon. Of course, after Clay announced that he planned to file as a conscientious objector, there was little talk of any kind at the Reverend White's dinner table. For that matter, there was little talk at all in the rectory.

Clay filed his appeal with the draft board. His mother worked her garden or sat by herself in the dark basement "cooling" herself. The Reverend White spent more time than ever in his study with his books preparing his Sunday sermons that espoused love and peace while rallying the flock to do their bit to wipe out the Krauts, the Wops, and the Japs. Especially those sneak-attacking Japs. Clay's mother dutifully nodded her head and maintained her smile all throughout the Sunday morning service. When the family returned home for their Sunday meal, the smile was put away with the hat and gloves, leaving sharp cracks in her makeup. At the table, the Reverend White complained about the elders and their wives, a subject his wife had always enjoyed, but now she showed scant interest.

Chuck continued to write letters home, regaling Clay with tales of weekend passes, booze, sporting girls, and the occasional Navy chump he cold-cocked for no particular reason while walking down the street. After he finished Basic, Chuck wrote that he volunteered for specialized training. Because of the censors, he couldn't elaborate. He couldn't name his new base or even speculate about when he might be ready to ship out or whether he would be assigned to the European or Pacific theater. It was so hush-hush that he wouldn't even be allowed to come home for the customary leave awarded to personnel before embarking overseas. It was just as well, he wrote, he had no interest in seeing his parents. As for Clay, someday, when the war was over, maybe they'd get together again. That was the last letter Clay received from Chuck. Clay kept all of them, bundled up with a piece of twine.

As he awaited fresh word from the Draft Board, Clay didn't bother to intercept the mail, and one day he found a letter from the Selective Service waiting for him on the side table by the front door. Again, it had already been opened. Clay soon learned that the state board had agreed to grant his request for a hearing. He turned to see his mother in the doorway of the kitchen watching him read it.

On the day of his interview, Clay took the earliest bus to Lancaster, where he connected with a train to Harrisburg. Dressed in his best Sunday suit, he carried a satchel that contained a Bible for appearance sake and an apple for a snack. He ate the apple on the bus, and while waiting in the lobby of the federal building in Harrisburg, he clutched the book. When called to the board room, he tucked the Bible to his heart, and followed the secretary down the hall.

Five men comprised the state draft board. They sat behind a long mahogany table beneath a mammoth reproduction of "Washington Crossing the Delaware."

"You may be seated, Mr. White."

Positioned ten feet from the table was an armless wooden chair. Clay's footsteps echoed in the chamber as he approached, sat down, leaned his satchel against a leg of the chair, and rested the Bible on his lap.

"Are we to understand that you brought no witnesses?"

"Not at this particular time, no sir."

"There is no other time, young man."

"Yes sir."

"Very well. Can you tell the board, Mr. White, when you first became aware of your moral opposition to war?"

"There was never a precise moment. My father is a minister —"

"Yes, we're well aware of that."

"The first thing I remember is my father reciting the Ten Commandments, one of which, of course, is 'Thou Shalt Not Kill.'"

"Can we assume you have kept that commandment?"

"Of course, yes sir."

"Have you kept the other nine commandments as well?"

"As best I can. But we have all sinned and fallen short of the glory of God."

"Naturally. Now let us pose a hypothetical to you, Mr. White. Say, you pay a visit to your grandmother and you walk in to find a prowler with a knife to her throat. There's also a gun handy. What would you do, Mr. White?"

"I don't know. Who does? And really that's a question of personal defense and has nothing to do with opposing war."

The door cracked open and a secretary leaned in. "Excuse me, gentlemen, but Mr. White's father has just arrived."

The Reverend White was waved in, and the secretary pulled a chair from a row against one wall, placing it next to Clay. The Reverend White sat down without looking at Clay.

"It's a pleasure to have you with us today, Reverend." The tone of the Board now took on more of a deferential timbre. "We all know why we are convened today. To substantiate your son's moral opposition to serving in the military."

"Yes, I understand."

"He says that you impressed upon him the need to adhere to the ten commandments, expressly, 'Thou shalt not kill.'"

"That is correct."

"May we ask if you taught him that such a doctrine applies to wartime situations in which the very existence of our country is at stake?"

"I did not."

"No?"

"I did, however, teach him to always follow the dictates of his heart. No one, not a father, not a minister, is privy to another's relationship with God. We may suspect, but we can never know. Thus, when my son tells me that God tells him that he should not serve in the military, I must take him at his word."

"Do you trust his word, sir?"

Reverend White paused to look at Clay and then returned his attention to the Board. "I do. I trust the word of my son."

"Very good then. You'll be notified of our decision in the mail."

The Board and the Reverend White engaged in a little parting chitchat. Clay was certain now that he would receive his CO status. His father had given him the seal of approval, and that was all the Board really wanted. There were plenty of young boys who could serve. Throwing a few fish back in the pond wasn't going to make any difference. And in a way, it made the game seem fair.

Without speaking to one another, Clay and his father left the conference room and walked to the elevator. While they waited, Clay said softly, "Dad, I just want you to know —"

"I don't want to hear it." The Reverend White kept his eyes on the dial above the elevator doors that indicated the current location of the car. "You got what you wanted. Now we're through. I want you out of the rectory. Today. I don't care where you go. I don't care what happens to you. From this moment forward, as far as I'm concerned, you are no longer my son. You cease to exist in my eyes."

The doors to the elevator lurched open and an attendant said, "Anyone need to get off before the lobby?" The Reverend White and Clay stood in opposite corners of the car. At the next floor, a group of young men filed in. Wearing varsity sweaters from the same high school, they were loud and excited, bragging about how they were going to personally string up Tojo. When the elevator reached the lobby, they allowed the Reverend White to make his exit, but inadvertently pinned Clay to the back of the car until his father had left the building.

When Clay returned home later in the day after another long bus ride, no one was home. On his bed, he found a new suitcase, a $100 bill, and a note in his father's hand saying that his mail would be forwarded to the YMCA in Lancaster.

Clay packed the suitcase and hitchhiked to Lancaster, where he paid for a bed in the common room of the YMCA. In a few days, Clay received his camp assignment: Camp No. 32, West Campton. It was located in the White Mountains of New Hampshire, its purpose to support the undermanned U.S. Forest Service. Clay took a train to North Conway, New Hampshire, a quaint tourist town that mostly catered to skiers in the winter. It was now late summer and only a handful of passengers stepped off the train. All of them piled into a woody station wagon sent by the work camp, a forty-minute ride from the depot. No one said a word the entire trip.

23

"You need help with something?" Clay turned to see some bored kid behind a register at the WaWa calling to him. "You okay?"

Clay said he was fine and opened a glass door to one of the refrigerated cases. He removed a bottle of water, and carried it to a cashier at the front of the WaWa store. When he saw the price digitally displayed—how he missed those old clanging cash registers—Clay was stunned. It had to be a mistake, but of course it wasn't. The kid behind the register had scanned the bottle, and the price was what it was. Clay didn't bother to argue, just left the bottle on the counter, and walked out of the store without his water.

God, a trained goat could be a store clerk. Back in the day, you had to have a head on your shoulders and some ambition to run a cash register. Stoller had this guy, Minor was his name, who worked the register at his main store. Minor was a magician with a cash register who took pride in his work. His thumb, fingers, and the palm of his right hand attacked the register keys while his left hand sorted the goods. There was a rhythm and music to the process, like Buddy Rich on the drums. And when the total popped up and that cash drawer rang open, Minor calculated the change as fast as a Univac machine, but unlike a Univac, he could bag. He snapped open a paper sack with the flip of his wrist and filled it before customers had time to reach for their wallet or dip into their purse. In a blur he made change and slammed shut the register drawer. Now, that was somebody happy to have a job and proud to do it the best way he could. Not like these kids working in the WaWa or Starbucks, who couldn't figure out the proper change in their heads if you gave them an hour, who didn't see their job as something worth doing well, but more like an insult, an interruption of their day.

Clay had never exchanged a word with Minor, but they knew each other by sight. Clay was counting on that as he sat in the diner across the street from Stoller's quick store. While eating breakfast, Clay watched Minor work the register. He read the latest about the Phillies in the Saturday *Inquirer* and kept an eye out for Stoller, waiting for him to leave. Clay forgot more about the 1950 Phillies than he'd ever know about the current team. It had been an exciting time for the city, but it also tested your nerves. With just fifteen games left in the season, the Whiz Kids had looked like a lock for the pennant, but since then, things had gone south. The Dodgers whittled the lead down to two games, and were now set to host the Phillies for the final weekend in Brooklyn. If the Dodgers won tonight and again on Sunday, the two teams would meet in a best-of-three playoff series, but if it got to that point, nobody believed an inexperienced team like the Phillies, with most of their starting pitchers sidelined for one reason or another, stood much of a chance. They had to win one of the last two games of the regular season.

Clay was so caught up in the story about that day's game, he almost missed Stoller leaving the store. Clay was lucky to look up at the last moment to catch a glimpse of Stoller stepping into his car. Seconds later, Stoller drove away. Clay folded his paper, finished his breakfast, and paid his check. He then crossed the street and entered the store where Minor was ringing up a customer.

"I think I left my lighter in the boss's office." Having received a nod in recognition from Minor, Clay walked to the back.

Clay sat at Stoller's desk and removed a pair of straightened paperclips from his pocket. He inserted them into the desk lock and seconds later was opening the side drawer where he had seen Stoller place the manila folder of blackmail notes. Clay quickly found the folder and opened it on his lap to find four pieces of light blue paper. Typed on two of the sheets in capital letters was the word "BETTENDORF." Another read "BETTENDORF. $5,000. INSTRUCTIONS TO FOLLOW." The final sheet listed the steps Stoller was to follow to make the payment to a safety deposit box, just like Stoller had told Clay when they had first met.

Less than a minute after entering the store, Clay was leaving. He held up a lighter to show Minor, shoved open the front door, and walked around the block to where his car was parked.

Bettendorf. Years later, Clay was walking the night streets of Philadelphia wondering why that name sounded familiar. He had a keycard in his hand. Room 809, the Hotel Windsor. Was that where he was going? Was that who he was supposed to meet? Bettendorf. Clay remembered driving somewhere after he read those notes in Stoller's store. It was to Pembroke's estate. He drove there straight away after leaving Stoller's store, pulled up to the front gate, and blew his horn. A negro came out to park his car, while another member of the help escorted Clay a few hundred yards to a shooting field. Clay was informed that Pembroke was doing a little skeet shooting. Ahead, Clay saw a half-circle of stations laid out between a pair of concrete houses from which the targets were launched. When they reached the houses, Clay was handed off to yet another domestic, this one wearing a white jacket who asked Clay what he cared to drink. Clay turned the corner to find Pembroke sipping on a tall glass of iced tea. A sprig of mint tickled his mustache. He was wearing a green barn jacket with deep pockets to hold shells, clutching the barrel of a break-action shotgun that was cracked open and balanced over one shoulder.

"I'm glad you could make it, Mr. White." In one quick motion, Pembroke snapped shut the shotgun, placed it in a rack with half a dozen others, and offered his hand to Clay. "Do you shoot?"

"If I have to."

"Have you ever done any sport shooting?"

"Most of it was sporting. I thought so, anyway."

"Very good. Perhaps you would care to join me in some target shooting. Do you prefer trap or skeet?"

"Either one's fine."

"I prefer skeet. The crossing shots."

"The double-crossing shots."

"Keeps the mind sharp."

Pembroke allowed Clay to select a gun from the rack. He then handed him two boxes of shells, which Clay emptied in the side pockets of his gray suit. While they took some practice shots from station 8, Pembroke talked about the history of the land on which they stood and how some Welshmen had named it after their native county, Merionethshire.

"It eventually took the name Merion Township," Pembroke said. "It was later divided by a railroad spur called the Main Line of Public Works, creating Upper and Lower Merion. On the southern edge of those tracks Philadelphia's wealthy built their homes. And that is why, my friend, Lower Merion is called the Main Line.

"I get the point," Clay said. "You were born on the right side of the tracks."

"I didn't mean to insinuate anything. It's just good to know your roots."

"If you have any."

Pembroke hit dead center on all of his practice shots. Clay, on the other hand, trailed slightly behind the targets, lucky at first to clip the back side. He soon improved his aim and agreed to step to the first station to begin shooting in earnest. Clay was given the honors. He planted his foot at twelve o'clock, raised his gun, and called, "Pull!" A pair of targets were launched one after the other, their paths intersecting between the trap houses, one high, one low. Clay pivoted to track the first target and as the barrel overtook it, he fired, exploding the target into red dust. He then swung to pick up the second target, destroying it as well.

"Nice." Pembroke stepped up for his shots and quickly dispatched a pair of targets.

"Any time you feel like getting to the point," Clay said, "don't let me stop you."

"I took you for the blunt type." Pembroke broke open his shotgun and picked out two spent shells. Without looking up, he said, "You should know I love my wife dearly."

"Glad to hear it."

"But I'm afraid I've been a bit of a fool."

"If it wasn't for foolish husbands and jealous wives, I'd be slinging hash."

"It's far from uncommon for a man in my position to enjoy . . . a dalliance."

"I would think it's almost expected on the Main Line. Like keeping a whipping boy for the kids."

"My wife has been a wonderful mother to my children—"

"I know, you made a terrible mistake."

"The very least a wife deserves is respect."

"I'm guessing that opinion is not shared by the cupcake in question."

"You make it sound so distasteful."

"I'm also guessing she doesn't know her place. I'm guessing she might want to take your wife's place."

"Perhaps that's the gist of it."

"You've tried to break it off, but the usurper— I've been working on my vocabulary—she lacks the manners to take a hint and make a graceful hike. No, she shows up at the house, a barbarian banging on the gates. Maybe she starts telephoning the house. That's the usual next move. Get the wife on the horn and say something that cuts to the quick. 'Just tell your husband he left his socks and garters under the bed. Don't worry, I'll be up late if he wants to come fetch them.'"

"In fact, she did ring the house the other night."

"Luckily you managed to intercept the call."

"That's right."

"But it was a close shave."

"Too close."

Clay took his position at the next station, shattered his set of targets, and stepped aside for Pembroke. "So why are you telling me this? Maybe because there's other parties involved here. Maybe your wife. Maybe my client."

"Yes, that's the sticky part. We're both men of the world, Mr. White. I hope we can talk openly."

"I can listen."

"Perhaps we can help one another. I know a lot of people. A recommendation from me could prove highly beneficial for someone in your line of work, provided of course..."

"I keep Stoller in the dark."

"You have so far. Obviously you plan on using that information to your advantage at some point."

"That point being now?"

"As you say."

"And the lady who likes to make late night calls? Is there something you'd like done there as well?"

"Just make it stop."

"That's a popular service these days. What makes you think she'll listen to me?"

"I doubt she will."

"Do you want me to threaten her?"

"I don't need to know the particulars. Of course I'll pay you your usual rate. And a bonus for good work."

Pembroke called for his targets. Hit one, missed the other.

"Bad luck, old boy."

"So do we have an understanding?" Pembroke broke open his shotgun.

"Maybe I'm a little slow. There are a lot of things I still don't understand."

"Such as?"

"Bettendorf."

"I beg your pardon?"

"Bettendorf. That mean anything to you?"

"No. Should it?"

"Just wondering."

"Is there anything else?"

"There is one other thing. Who killed Inspector Ellis?"

"Ellis? The man killed himself. It was in all the papers."

"Funny, but I saw you talking to Ellis not five minutes before the end. Looked like a bit of an argument. And I didn't see him shoot himself. I watched a little guy pull the trigger."

"Maybe you should have told your story to the police."

"But you're glad I didn't. Because I would have brought up your name. Not to mention the Hosiery Corporation of America. Maybe that one rings a bell."

"This situation has become terribly muddled, Mr. White."

"Perhaps you can enlighten me."

"Inspector Ellis was just as confused as you are. And as I am, frankly. He was under the impression that I wanted to prevent this hosiery company from constructing a factory. He thought I was threatening to reveal some information that would ruin his life. I shall repeat what I told him. I know nothing about this company. I don't care about this company and whether they build a new plant or not."

"Do you know who sold the company that piece of land?"

"No, I'm afraid I do not."

"What if I told you it was your business partner Stoller?"

"Bully for him."

"You're not upset that he cut you out of the deal?"

"Why should I be? We've made ample money together."

"Not to mention, you're bedding his wife."

"Not to mention. Is there anything else you need to know?"

"That's enough." Clay walked back to the gun rack.

"We've barely begun shooting," Pembroke called.

"When the targets start shooting back let me know."

"Do we have a deal, Mr. White?"

Clay slotted the shotgun in the rack and dumped the shells from his pockets onto a table.

"Do we have a deal?"

Without answering, Clay walked back to the front gate. He asked for his car and while one of the help left to bring it to the gate, Pembroke's smiling wife approached from the house looking just like that happy picture in the *Inquirer*. She was dressed for riding, carrying a crop in one hand and a black, crushed velvet riding helmet tucked under the opposite arm.

"Finished shooting so soon?" she said. "I'm Victoria, Monty's wife. And your name is?"

"White. Clay White."

"A pleasure to meet you." She held out a hand and gave his a squeeze. Clay felt a folded piece of paper pressed into his hand. He said nothing as she looked him in the eye and commented on the fine weather they were having. They continued to smile at one another as Clay's car arrived. The gates were opened to allow him to leave the estate. He drove until he was out of sight.

Clay pulled over to the side of the road and unfolded the note: *I must see you at 4:00. V.* Below was the address for a private boat house on the Schuylkill River.

24

Clay considered the red awning of the Hotel Windsor across the street. The time had come to settle all of this. Whatever this was. Clay didn't have to make sense of it, just fulfill his assignment. He had watched his guy, this J, for days. He watched him leave his apartment and walk to his shop where he worked from early morning to early evening. J looked like a million other guys in the city, but he was the only one Clay was supposed to take care of. Of course, Clay should have already finished the job. There was no need to study the mark so deeply. It was what it was. Clay didn't need to make sense of it. He didn't need to know the reasoning behind the decision. J needed to be dealt with, and Clay was the tool at hand. He could have finished the job the first evening he followed the man home from his shop. He didn't have to make it look like a robbery gone wrong or an accident or anything at all. He just needed to do it. But he didn't.

Clay crossed the street to the Hotel Windsor and looked at the keycard tucked in his hand. Room 809.

J was waiting, right? Finally, Clay could meet the man he was supposed to kill and... then what? Ask his forgiveness? Persuade J—and himself—that this sacrifice was necessary? For what?

To his left, Clay could see Philadelphia's City Hall, crowned by a statue of William Penn, King's charter in hand. Wasn't Clay supposed to be in New York's Lower East Side? This was all wrong. He stood on the sidewalk outside the hotel lobby, staring at the key card. Who was he meeting if not J? He was important, whoever he was, and he was in room 809.

Clay clutched the keycard, determined to hold onto his intent. He entered the lobby unnoticed by the night clerk and walked across the small lobby to the elevator bank. Room 809. Assailed by random thoughts and memories, Clay stared at the keycard and whispered to himself, "809, 809." When the car arrived, Clay entered, quickly punched the button for the eighth floor, and returned his eyes to the key card. Just as the doors were about to close, a hand reached in to trigger the sensor. A moment later, a women with red hair and a leather portfolio entered the car. She looked familiar. Clay was certain he had seen her before. He slipped the keycard in his jacket pocket and tried to remember who she was. And then he had it. It was that night after it became apparent that Steve would never emerge from his coma caused by that ambulance crew. The time had come to think about the estate. And the future of HCA. Clay was vaguely aware of the situation when one evening Vivian and a pair of lawyers—one man, one woman—came to fetch him. The woman had red hair just like the woman in the elevator. Clay was certain it was the same woman. What did she want now?

That other time, Vivian had said she needed family with her. That's why the lawyers picked him up on the way to Vivian's house. Clay remembered waiting in the living room before Ryan and his wife Phyllis showed up. On their heels was Tom Pembroke. Vivian asked him what he was doing there.

"I'm sorry," Phyllis said. "I might have mentioned it to him. Tom's a sweet boy. He's just trying to be supportive."

The group marched up the stairs to the master bedroom and arrayed themselves while Vivian lifted a painting, an original Wyeth, off its hook, to reveal a wall safe. The male lawyer stepped forward with an envelope in his hand, opened it, removed a slip of paper, placed a pair of reading glasses on his nose, and while glancing at the paper twisted the dial of the safe. He pulled open the door and then stepped aside to allow everyone to pass by and observe that the safe was empty.

"It would appear," the lawyer finally said, "that Mr. Hess has left no will."

"And that means what exactly?" Phyllis asked.

"Under Pennsylvania law, his wife is entitled to the entire estate."

"There is one other matter," Ryan said. Phyllis gripped Ryan's one good hand. "A buy-sell agreement Steve and I signed."

Ryan explained that in the event that either he or Steve should die, the survivor had the right to buy out the other's interest in HCA at fair market value. Both men assumed that neither Vivian nor Phyllis would want to run a panty hose company.

"How much do you think fair market value is?" Vivian asked.

"Four dollars a share, I should say. Which would come to about $4 million."

"Make it $10 a share."

"I advise you to say nothing more," said the attorney.

"It's not up to us to set a price," Ryan said. "I was just stating my opinion. As part of the agreement, the price is to be determined by an arbitrator, a so-called wise man Steve and I both agreed upon."

"Sounds like a low-ball offer to me," Pembroke said, addressing his comment at Phyllis.

"Sometimes even sweet boys need to keep quiet."

"Steve came to me when his parents died," Ryan explained. "He knew he wasn't ready to run the business but was smart enough to know his inexperience could jeopardize the health of the company and the extent of his wealth. I was well past retirement age. We simply struck a deal that was in both of our best interests."

"You already own nearly half the business, right?" Again, it was Pembroke talking to Phyllis.

"And I greatly increased its value," Ryan replied. "Steve never complained, at any rate. The fact remains, we made an agreement."

"I'm confused," Pembroke said.

"That's obvious." Phyllis's voice was growing less pleasant.

"Why didn't you just offer to buy out Steve? Maybe you didn't offer enough. It's not like he wanted to run the company anymore than I would."

"We didn't realized this was about you," Phyllis said.

"No more than it's about you."

"I think my wife is getting tired." Ryan gripped Phyllis' elbow. "Perhaps we should call it a night."

They left the bedroom and descended the stairs. With the exception of Clay, Vivian saw everyone off at the door. The last to go was Pembroke, but before he left, he said softly to the young widow in waiting, "I'm here."

"I know you are."

"No really . . . I'm here."

Steve died three days later and immediately Vivian was appointed administratrix of the estate. She then informed the county probate officials that her husband died without a will, setting in motion her claim on Steve's estate. At the same time, Ryan's lawyers went to court to enforce his buy-sell agreement and call in the stock.

Clay begged her to keep him informed, to tell him all the details. It was complicated but for Clay it was a relief, something to fill his brain besides bad memories. And unlike his life, it made sense to him.

"The doctor says it's actually good for your cognition," his granddaughter said. "And it's good for me to talk it out."

"So what happens next?" he asked. They were out for a walk at a nearby park.

"Well everybody is saying that the market value of HCA is $4.5 million, and Ryan offered five, so my lawyers want me to accept rather than go to court and contest the buy-sell agreement."

"Good idea," Clay said.

"Are they kidding? Is that it?" It was young Pembroke, who was making a habit of showing up in Vivian's life. "They're all on the same side. The HCA accountants all work for Ryan. And he hand-picked the arbitrator."

"Maybe you're right, but $5 million is a lot of money," Vivian said.

"It's not as much as you think. You'll barely get by on five. Trust me on this one. My family's been there, done that."

"I have other assets, other possibilities."

"You mean your grandpa here? I'm sure you're in his will, but . . . who knows when?"

"My lawyers tell me to settle."

"Maybe you need to get new lawyers."

"They're well respected. They never lose."

"They never try to win! They talk their clients into settling. You can't tell me they don't get a little bonus from the other side for rolling over."

"They're honest."

"They're not that honest. Listen, I did a little investigation of my own. A buddy of mine is a financial advisor and I asked him to do some calculations about how much HCA is worth based on reported sales and the estimated value of other assets. He says your share of the stock is worth $25 million. Easy! You should be asking for fifty, not taking five to avoid a fight. You probably won't get fifty, but you'll probably get closer to twenty-five than you will to five. Now you're talking about some money."

"I don't know. . ."

"I'm the only one without a dog in this fight. Steve was my friend and I just want you to be treated right."

"I appreciate that."

"I said I'd be here for you . . . and I still am . . . I always will be."

"What do you think, Grandpa?"

"Has the ballgame started yet?"

The next day Vivian fired her lawyers.

"I want to apologize," Clay told the red-haired woman in the elevator.

"Excuse me?" she said.

"My granddaughter should have listened to your advice."

"Are you feeling okay, sir?"

Now that he looked closer, this woman in the elevator was much younger than the redheaded lawyer from that night. Clay apologized for his mistake, insisted he was feeling fine, and refused the woman's offer of assistance. She exited the elevator and Clay continued on, although unsure now of his destination. The doors opened on the eighth floor and he stepped out. It was as good a floor as any. He slowly walked down the hall, struggling to remember where he was going and why. Hell, who was he, for that matter?

"I'm Clay White," he muttered to himself. "My father was a minister. He and my mother never forgave me for not fighting in the war."

That's right. He was Clay White. The CO. He had to hold onto whatever facts he could. He sat out the war, along with all the other CO's at the work camp. It was a crazy quilt collection of men and faiths or non-faiths. Clay kept to himself, mostly thinking about home, wishing he was back in Pennsylvania. He found himself missing his parents and figured they were probably missing him as well. He expected that soon a letter would arrive from his father, who would have tracked down Clay's whereabouts to reconcile their differences. He was a peacemaker, right? He'd welcome back the prodigal son. Clay became so convinced that his father would write, that he wrote a reply to have ready for the post. He wrote a second, then a third letter that he never sent while waiting for a letter from his father that never came. He described camp life and his fellow COs. There was a group of bearded professors and be-speckled writers who engaged in passionate never-ending debates on every possible subject. Although they never came to blows, they seemed continually on the verge of violence, red-faced and gesticulating from sunup to lights out. There was also a large contingent of brawny farmers and reticent woodsmen who shared their own topics of interest. Then there were the Molokans, Russians who were supposedly a sect like the Amish, but one that had a decided mean streak. While they insisted that it was against their faith to kill, they were not above, indeed they enjoyed, kicking in someone's teeth on occasion. Not much provocation was required. They were kept in a side camp where they could brawl among themselves. The din from their barracks was constant and audible for miles.

Clay wrote to his father that although it was primarily a firefighting camp, there were few fires to worry about in the damp Northeast. Mostly the fires were caused by lightening strikes and quickly contained by digging trenches to isolate the flames. Once the digging was completed, the men sat around and kept watch to make sure the fire didn't jump the trench.

Some of the men in camp volunteered for medical experiments to relieve the boredom and maybe help change the world for the better. Clay was one of those who agreed to live on a diet lacking in Vitamin C or protein, like many of the refugees created by the war. He kept his father informed about all the details. For several weeks the subjects ate carefully prescribed meals. They were then given backpacks filled with rocks and sent to climb a mountain. At the top, researchers were waiting to take blood samples. After three months, Clay found himself noticeably weaker, his gums felt soft, and his skin looked pasty. He was also very hungry and irritable. When the experiment came to a sudden close one day, Clay and the other subjects were told nothing about what had been learned from their sacrifice. For that matter, they weren't even thanked. They were CO's after all. Serving as test subjects was the least they could do while others fought and died for their country.

The letters Clay never sent to his father began to accumulate. He stashed them in a wood case with a top, an old shipping container for work gloves, that he kept under his cot. More than once, Clay discovered the box had been opened and someone had leafed through the letters, probably looking for something of value. After a while, as the letters filled the box, nobody bothered to look inside anymore. When he ran out of things to write about in camp, Clay began to wonder how things had gone wrong between him and his parents. He wrote about the time his cousin drew the ugly picture of his mother. He gave a full confession about the detective stories and the whole story behind his decision, if you could call it a decision, to become a conscientious objector.

After two years at West Campton, Clay asked to be transferred to a different assignment. He was sent to the Cheltenham School for Boys in Maryland to work with juvenile delinquents and put out a different kind of fire. Clay took his crate of letters, paper, and pens—his only real possessions besides clothes and a shaving kit—and continued to write letters to his father he would never send.

25

Clay was startled when a door swung open and a young woman stepped into the hotel hallway, spotted him, and whispered, "What do you think you're doing? Get in here!" She clutched him by the arm and pulled him into a room. While she locked the door behind them, Clay spotted a pair of legs protruding from a bathroom at the end of a short hallway. Lifeless legs.

"Who is that?" Clay asked.

"I can't believe I fell asleep. How long were you gone?"

"Is he … is he dead?"

"Please. I can't take any more of this."

"This is a set up. A honey trap."

"Stop it! I'm your granddaughter. Look in the right pocket of your jacket."

Clay reached into his pocket and pulled out a keycard with "#809" written on it. He had seen the same number on the door of this room. Whoever was setting him up was good. Very good.

"So what's the story supposed to be told here?" Clay tossed the keycard on a side table. "I was jealous. I found you two together. In a rage I shot him coming out of the bathroom. I'm guessing my prints are all over that gat on the floor."

"I'm your granddaughter. Vivian. Try to at least remember that much. I'm your granddaughter."

Well, if this was Clay's granddaughter, and there was every reason—and no reason—to believe it was, Clay pegged her as a calmer sort than her grandmother. Or maybe a better actress. Clay was the one who broke the tragic news to Grandma about her first husband.

"It can't be true," his soon-to-be wife murmured, head in hands.

"Grandpa, Grandpa. Look at me. You're drifting on me."

"Vivian?"

"That's right. That's better. It's Vivian. We're waiting for the police. There was an accident. A death. It has nothing to do with you. You need to trust me and come sit down and wait until the police can deal with this."

It made no sense, but Clay believed the girl was playing it straight. And he was actually tired. He allowed her to lead him around the corner to an easy chair covered with yellow Post-Its. He sat down and began inspecting the notes. Barrett. Box top. Bettendorf.

Bettendorf. It meant something. But what? Clay felt this wasn't the first time he had asked that question. He had puzzled over it years ago. He remembered driving to the main branch of the Free Library over on Logan Square. Clay had asked a librarian if the word Bettendorf meant anything to him.

"How do you mean, exactly?"

"Is it a person, place, or thing?"

"If I had to hazard a guess, I would say a place. A town in Iowa along the Mississippi."

"Do you know if they have a newspaper?"

A few minutes later, the librarian was providing Clay with the phone number to the *Davenport Democrat & Leader*, a newspaper that served the area from nearby Davenport, Iowa. Clay returned to his office and called the paper, identifying himself as a Philadelphia police detective, asking if he could speak with the person in charge of the newspaper's morgue, where the paper kept its back issues. Once connected to a guy named Benson, Clay asked if there had been any unsolved murders or robberies that took place in Bettendorf in the past twenty years or so.

"You mean other than the Steinlauf killing?" Benson said. He didn't need to consult any press clippings to give Clay the lowdown on the Steinlauf killing. Anybody living within a hundred miles knew the story. Steinlauf was an area farmer who didn't do much farming. He certainly sold plenty of livestock, but he didn't raise any of it.

"He was a rustler and a thief and a rural thug," Benson said. "Everybody was afraid of him, especially the local constable."

Steinlauf apparently took what he wanted and got away with it for years, thanks in no small part to the smart lawyer he hired across the river in Moline, Illinois. "People tried to have the law deal with Steinlauf," Benson said, "but after he managed to beat three or four raps, they gave up and just hoped his wild ways—all the drinking and visits to Chicago cat houses and back-alley brawls—would finally catch up to him. Only it seemed like they never would."

Steinlauf was a family man in his own way. Had a wife in Bettendorf, and according to rumor he kept another somewhere in Illinois, or maybe Wisconsin. Maybe in both states. There were assorted girlfriends as well. He wasn't a handsome man, but he had a way of getting what he wanted. His Iowa wife, a pretty but meek woman who rarely left the farm, gave him a son. A few years later, a daughter followed, but his wife died giving birth to the girl. Steinlauf was now left to raise two children by himself. Of course, he didn't do much of the parenting, leaving that to a succession of girlfriends, none of them the mothering type.

"Steinlauf believed in discipline. In fact, he enjoyed discipline," Benson said. Let the women coddle his offspring if they wanted to, he'd handle the belt. And he used it liberally. Mostly on the boy, and more regularly as the boy grew older. As for the girl, Steinlauf reserved a different way to keep her in check. Their offenses, of course, were more imaginary than real. Confined to the farm, what kind of trouble could they expect to find? Yet, somehow they found it, at least in the eyes of the ever watchful Steinlauf.

"Nobody was especially surprised," Benson said, "when Steinlauf was found one morning with his skull crushed under a pickup truck he was repairing."

Steinlauf drank a lot and was careless as hell. It appeared that he had been fixing a brake line, had jacked up one corner of the truck and removed a tire to get a better angle. He was lying under the truck when the flimsy jack that was holding it up worked its way free, and all that weight came crashing down on Steinlauf. Everyone in the county thought it less an accident than an act of divine deliverance.

"Maybe the constable chalked it up as an accident, but it wasn't his call and the county cops had other ideas," Benson said.

"What was their take?" Clay asked.

"Murder."

Too many details argued against an accident. There was a deep crescent cut in the ground that pointed like an arrow to where the jack was found about five feet from the truck. A few paces further in the grass, the county cops found a long-handled apple hook, ideal for pulling down branches to pluck out-of-reach apples— or yanking a jack out from under a truck.

"If that wasn't suspicious enough," Benson said, "somebody realized that Steinlauf's kids were missing."

In the beginning there was a thought that maybe some mystery person or gang had killed Steinlauf and taken his children, but that theory didn't seem to hold much water. Plenty of people had reason to kill Steinlauf, all of Bettendorf had cause for that matter, but no one would have an interest in abducting Steinlauf's teenage son and daughter after the guy was dead. No, the authorities suspected that the children, at least the son, had done the killing and run away. Maybe the boy did it and ran, and the girl, after she discovered her father dead, was afraid she'd get blamed and ran too. More likely, went the general thinking, they did it together and ran away together.

Nobody really blamed the kids for killing Steinlauf. He had abused them for years, they were underage, and they might have even beat the charges if they claimed they feared for their lives. But they had probably done the deed and then fled. The authorities had no choice but to report them as fugitives from the law. Nobody, however, took much interest in actually finding them, whether together or split up. Not the cops in Iowa, nor the cops anywhere else for that matter. It was still an open case, murder having no statute of limitations, and the authorities would mete out justice if called upon, but everybody figured justice had already been served.

"Any picture of the boy in the files?" Clay asked.

"I don't think so. They hardly went to school. Weren't allowed in town. And it's been so long. Can I ask why you're inquiring about the case? Is there a new lead?"

Rather than answer, Clay dropped the phone in the cradle to disconnect the call. He reached for his cigarettes, placed one between his lips. A good thirty seconds passed before he thought to light it. But it wasn't a cigarette, it was a pen Clay had picked up along with a Post-It pad. He wrote "Focus," peeled off the slip and found an open space on the chair arm to stick it.

Clay dropped his left arm and several notes tickled his arm. He removed one to read "Cheltenham." First Bettendorf, now Cheltenham. Was this some kind of scavenger hunt he was playing with his memory?

"Does 'Cheltenham' mean anything to you?" Clay asked the girl in the hotel room, his supposed granddaughter.

"You're driving me crazy, Grandpa."

That was all the hint he needed. Cheltenham was where they sent the crazy kids, although a lot of them were just troubled kids that were treated as if they were crazy. And it was where they sent CO's. It was a rougher world for kids in places like Cheltenham back in the day. Clay had tried to be different. For awhile anyway.

It took about two months before Clay struck his first child at Cheltenham. Clay wrote to his father that it was more a shove than an actual blow, but it was a start. The boys became less likely to talk back or disobey Clay, but they didn't actually change. Soon, one of them tried his luck and Clay clocked him. That earned Clay a little respect and more time passed before he struck another one of them. Eventually he began looking for a reason and was even willing to manufacture one to throw a boy up against a wall or toss a boy to the ground. No one complained. His father had to understand that was just the Cheltenham way.

The war, in the meantime, was going well for the Allies. It was obvious that it was only a matter of time before the war would come to an end, all the servicemen would come home and the CO's would be allowed to resume their normal lives. It was a prospect that Clay found disheartening. He had given no thought to what he wanted to do when he was free to go. Unlike returning soldiers, he would have no G.I. Bill for college. And who would hire him over someone who had served his country? He couldn't return home to his parents. He was dead to them. Despite the letters he continued to write, he knew that. And he was probably dead to everyone in town, who by this time knew he had gone CO.

Clay wished the war would last longer to give him more time to decide what he wanted to do with his life. He was disappointed that the Germans proved to be such pushovers. At least the Japanese kept things going into the summer of 1945, but then they folded, too. The war was over, church bells were ringing, people were in the streets celebrating. Clay thought that he would be free to simply walk out of the gates of Cheltenham, but it wasn't that simple. Nothing changed. He and the other CO's continued to work for free. Finally, a year after the war was over, word came down that the CO's were released from their obligation. It was more like they were being fired. They were told a bus would be ready to take them to the train station in the morning and they were expected to be on it.

Once again, Clay stood with his suitcase on a train platform, along with a wooden case tied up with a leather strap. This time he was headed for Philadelphia, a big city where he could lose himself in the crowd and try to make a life for himself.

26

"Where are the Goddamn police?" the girl in the room said.

"The police. Why?" Clay asked.

"You know, Grandpa. Barrett. In the bathroom. Oh Jesus, I can't stand this. I should have been clearer when I called 911. I should have said, 'There's been a murder.'"

"A murder?"

"They probably thought I was reporting a hotel bar fight or something."

Clay located a note on the chair. "Barrett: Murder Victim." He remembered now why he felt there was a crisis.

There was a light rapping at the door.

The girl looked at Clay. "The cops usually aren't so polite," he said. "You better see who it is."

"It was a suicide. Remember that, please, Grandpa."

Clay followed and watched her peer through the hotel room peephole. "Oh Jesus!"

"Who is it?"

"Phyllis."

"What does she want?" For that matter, who was she?

"How would I know what she wants, Grandpa? Should I just let her in and find out?"

Phyllis knocked again. "I can hear you in there."

Vivian cracked open the door. "This is not a good time."

"We can help. Please let me in. I'm sure we can work this out to everyone's satisfaction."

"Where's your husband?"

"Parking the car. He'll be up in a minute. We thought maybe you would listen to me first."

"I'm sorry, but you're wasting your time."

"Is something the matter, dear?"

"Do you always have to be so damn nosy?"

"Something is wrong."

"What makes you say that?"

"You have blood on your sleeve."

Clay laid his hand on Vivian's shoulder. "Just let her in."

A moment later, Phyllis was inside the room and asking questions. She wanted to know why Clay was there. She wanted to know about the blood. She wanted to know where Barrett was.

"Barrett is in the bathroom. He killed himself. That's where the blood comes from," Vivian said.

"What?" Phyllis marched to the bathroom but stopped short as soon as she caught a glimpse of the body. She turned to Clay. "You did this?"

"Did I?"

"You don't know? How could you not know?"

"I don't know."

"You're wasting your time, Phyllis. I told you Barrett killed himself." Vivian tugged Clay on the arm and again led him to the Lazy Boy.

"You have to call the police." Phyllis walked toward the phone. "And they're not going to buy the suicide story."

"They're on the way. Jesus, do you think we were going to just dump the body?"

"Clay, what happened really?"

"He doesn't remember."

"Does he remember anything?"

Clay did remember something. He remembered all those dinners he spent with his wife and Phyllis, his step mother-in-law (if there was such a thing), and her husband. She always had been a busybody. It didn't matter what the subject, she had an opinion. He and Ryan might talk about HCA, and Phyllis would weigh in. Actually she knew a lot about the business, more than Clay in fact, and he sat on the board of directors. She was the one responsible for HCA keeping up with the trends, moving to one-size-fits-all, quickly embracing spandex, adding tights to the lineup, incorporating Lycra, moving production to South Carolina, then sourcing the product from Haiti and China. Over the years, HCA had always remained ahead of the curve, and Clay knew it was due in no small measure to Phyllis. She persuaded her husband to diversify, to start publishing romance novels that they could promote with flyers that were sent out with the pantyhose. She suggested they rent out the mailing list and start using it to sell vitamins and aromatherapy candles. But she was still a pain in the ass.

"The kid just wanted some money. He would have walked away. You didn't have to shoot him."

"It's more complicated than that, Phyllis!" Although the woman was her great grandmother, Vivian had always called her Phyllis. And always treated her like a nuisance.

"I'm sorry, I thought we were family. I thought families worked together."

"Maybe some families do. Families that don't have members trying to steal from one another."

"Barrett is—was—a troubled boy."

"I was talking about you and your husband. I was talking about you two trying to steal the company from me."

"From you? What have you ever done for HCA that makes it your company? Have you so much as opened an envelope? Have you ever visited one of the plants where they make our product? Do you even know where they are? Do you know how the products are made?"

"They're made in China now. I know that much. And if it belonged to my husband, it belongs to me. And your husband is trying to steal it from me. That's all I need to know."

"Okay, I understand. But you don't want the company. You said so yourself. I'm sure we can find a price to make everybody happy . . . although Barrett's demise does complicate matters. And simplify them. Are you sure you don't remember anything, Clay?"

What Clay remembered was his wife fighting with Phyllis. What he remembered was his wife telling her one night to mind her own business and to stop acting like her mother when she really wasn't. As the years went on, they spent less time together. The dinners between the four of them became less frequent. Even at the end, when she was dying, his wife didn't want to see Phyllis. Only when she was too weak to protest, too weak to keep up the bickering, did she allow Phyllis into her sick room, to hold her hand and pass her final days together. It was Phyllis that was with her when she died, not Clay. He was watching a ballgame upstairs.

"Do you remember anything at all?" Phyllis asked.

"It was raining," Clay said.

It seemed like it rained a lot in Clay's life.

It was raining that other time, too. After Clay shot skeet with Pembroke and the guy's wife slipped him a note asking him to meet her at four at a boat house. It started to rain just as Clay arrived. That's what he remembered most. The rain. There was already a cream-colored Cadillac convertible parked under some trees where it couldn't be seen from the road. Clay pulled up next to it and stepped out of his Dodge. The license plate number on the Caddy caught his eye: 9DP36. It was a pure baseball combination and easy to remember: nine plus double play and Robert Roberts' uniform number 36. Hell, he remembered it all these years later. Clay walked over to the wooden boat house perched over the water and flanked by a slatted pier. The double front doors of the boat house led onto a porch, and an immediate set of steps fed into the river.

Clay called for Mrs. Pembroke. Receiving no reply, he walked up the steps to the boat house, onto the porch, and tried the door. It was unlocked. He opened the door and looked inside. It took a moment for his eyes to adjust to the darkness. Along the nearest wall were racks of sculls and oars. He heard a moan from a corner of the room on the opposite side of the door. He stepped into the room to see Lynne bound, gagged, and curled up on the floor, then felt someone clutch his shoulder, twist him, and strike him on the back of the head with something heavy.

Slowly Clay began to come around. His coughing helped. Smoke was quickly filling the boat house. He recognized the sound of a crackling fire, and opened his eyes to see orange flames interlaced between the sculls on the one wall. Lynne was not far away, struggling to free herself from the cords that lashed her ankles together and pulled her wrists behind her back. Clay got to his feet but stayed low to avoid the smoke filling the room as he scrambled to the front door. It opened outward but was locked and offered little play, jammed shut by something on the other side. He quickly sized up the room. Between the boards on the far side of the boat house he detected some sunlight. Clay caught Lynne by the wrists and pulled her to the light. Lying on his side, he back-heeled the wall until he broke through. As soon as he made a large enough hole, he shoved Lynne into the water below and quickly jumped in to pull her out and lift her onto the shore.

Clay's head throbbed and he was wobbly on his feet. Lynne was wet and shivering and still terrified. Both of them were unable to stop coughing, but neither wanted to stick around to watch the boat house burn or wait for the curious to arrive once the flames became apparent from the road. The Caddy was gone, but Clay's car was still under the trees where he left it protected from the rain. On the front seat he found a piece of paper. Written on it in pencil was "BLAME HER."

"What's that supposed to mean?" Lynne asked.

"Even when it comes to murder-suicide notes, I'm apparently a man of few words."

Clay drove quickly from the boathouse, keeping a constant eye on the rearview mirror. "Did you get a look at who did this?"

"It was that man from the other night."

"What man? What night?"

"The movies. The wolf you sent packing."

"Are you sure?"

"He asked how I liked the movies. So yeah, I'm sure."

"Did he say anything else?"

"No. He wasn't just some chaser. He was all business. He knew what he was doing. He grabbed me as I was getting into my car, and before I knew it I was gagged and dumped into his trunk. Then he tied me up and we waited for you in the boat house."

"A real gentle persuader."

"Who would do this to me? Who hired him?"

"If I had to guess," Clay said, "I'd say whoever sent me to find you."

"Who did?"

"I wish I knew. It was an anonymous tip."

"But you're going to find out, right?"

"Count on it. It's bad for business to get sapped and set on fire. Clients might think you're not up to the job."

They coughed and drove until they spotted a filling station where Clay bought some bottles of Dr. Pepper to soothe their throats. Clay sipped his soda while he drove.

"Bettendorf," he said.

"What?"

"Bettendorf. That mean anything to you?"

"What are you talking about?"

"What's it mean to you?"

"You think that's the guy who did this?"

"I don't know. Maybe."

Clay drove Lynne to her stepmother's place. They tried to tell Phyllis that they had been in an automobile accident and walked to a service station in the rain because no one would stop to pick them up. That's why they were so shook up. And wet. Phyllis didn't believe it and demanded to know the truth. Lynne told her that somebody had tried to kill them in a fire. Phyllis didn't believe that one either.

"Can you smell the smoke on our clothes?" Lynne said.

"What's that prove? You could have been camping."

"Fine, you really want to know the truth? I was out drinking and met someone, but he shows up like the good Boy Scout to drag me home, but we fell into a swimming pool. That's why we're so fucking wet."

"See, that wasn't so hard," Phyllis said.

Phyllis walked Clay to the front door and in a low voice asked him what had really happened.

"Somebody tried to set us on fire."

"Never mind." Phyllis smiled and closed the door.

After a quick change at home into another gray suit, Clay drove to Pembroke's estate. By the time he arrived the sun was setting. The help who had admitted him earlier in the day said that Mr. Pembroke was not in.

"I'm looking for Mrs. Pembroke, actually." Clay fanned a sawbuck.

"She's already left, suh."

"When do you expect her back?"

"Christmas perhaps."

"Where'd she go?"

"Paris. Her ship should be sailing about now, suh."

"Kind of a sudden trip."

"She's been planning it for weeks."

"Did she take her car?"

"Not likely, suh. It was stolen a few days ago."

"The light-colored Caddy convertible? The one with plate number 9DP36?"

"That's the car, but not the plate. I know it has NC in it. It always reminds me of where I'm from. North Carolina. Will that be all, suh?"

While he waited in his car, Clay listened to the radio account of the Phillies' game. He was pulled off the road some fifty yards from the lane that led to the boat house, tucked in between some bushes. Only someone who slowed down and was looking could spot where he was hidden. The area was quiet now, although a fire truck from the local volunteer company paid a brief visit to make sure nothing had flared up. Because the boat house had collapsed into the river, that was not very likely to happen.

Clay was hungry and a bit annoyed as he watched and waited. He left the motor running so he wouldn't drain the battery listening to the game, but it wasn't worth the gas money. The game fell apart in the fifth. The Phils began to rally, but the Dodgers put the game away in the eighth.

Clay was listening to the final outs of the game when he noticed a car approach the lane to the boat house, switch off its lights, and swing down to the river bank. Clay killed his engine, grabbed the revolver that was lying on the front seat, ran across the road, and scrambled through a stand of trees to the boat house where a cream-colored Caddy convertible sat idling with the top up.

Clay approached the Caddy low and from behind, and quickly opened the door with one hand while striking the driver on the side of the face with the butt of his revolver. The guy was stunned, and Clay was able to drag him out of the car by the shoulder of his suit coat. Even though it was dark, Clay recognized the guy from the night at the movies. Clay kicked him in the side, searched him and found a pistol, then pulled him to his feet by the back of his collar and pushed him to the water's edge. He knocked him down again and kneed his back, forcing his head near the water.

"Surprised nobody reported a murder, just a fire? I guess you needed to see for yourself. Well, how do you like the view?" Clay gripped him by the hair and forced his head under water.

It didn't take long to find out his name was Harris. He was a private op hired by Mrs. Pembroke because she suspected her husband was cheating on her. Usually dames hired him to set up a divorce, but not this time. The lady liked her situation and just wanted Harris to scare off the competition. Harris said that's what he would have done that night at the movies if Clay hadn't decided to butt in.

"You made it personal, bub."

Mrs. Pembroke didn't know what she was setting up with that note she passed to Clay. She probably thought Clay was just another blackmailing private eye who needed a lesson.

"Scaring off people seems to be a house specialty," Clay said. "Only you prefer the permanent solution."

"Blame yourself, bub."

"I know. I made it personal."

Clay stood up, shot Harris in the back of his thigh with his own gun, and walked away, leaving the guy cursing and writhing in pain. By the time he reached his Dodge and switched on the radio, the Phillies' game was over. They had lost. The pennant was all coming down to the final game of the season on Sunday.

27

Phyllis was on her cell phone with a 911 dispatcher, making sure the cops were actually on the way. As she returned the phone to her purse, there was a rap on the door. It was her husband, finished parking the car. Ryan was told about the accident. He was not especially surprised, just went to take a look at the body, showing about as much emotion as a plumber arriving to check out a leak. "Once an op always an op," Clay said.

"How'd you ever get into the game?" Ryan asked.

That was a good question. What was the story? After the war and he was finally released from Cheltenham, Clay had moved to Philadelphia and looked for a job where they weren't overly particular about a guy's background and wouldn't pry. Clay began making deliveries for a local pharmacy. He stayed less than a month. It was just the first in a string of mindless, dead-end jobs that paid just enough money to rent a drably-furnished room that offered nothing more than a bed, a chair, a dresser, a hotplate, and cockroaches. There was also a small writing table, but Clay never used it. As soon as his days as a conscientious objector were over, he stopped writing letters to his father.

Clay waited tables at a few places but never for very long, manned a cash register at any number of businesses, worked as night auditor at a hotel, tried his hand at selling bronzed baby shoes in the suburbs, threw out his back working for a moving company, handed out fliers, and on more than one occasion sold his blood to buy groceries.

It was after one of those occasions when he was reduced to selling his blood that Clay met his childhood friend Chuck on the streets of Philadelphia. It was actually Chuck who recognized Clay. Chuck hardly looked like the same fleshy kid Clay remembered. He was now muscular with a bull neck, thick chest, and painful grip.

Chuck suggested they find a bar, have a drink, and catch up. Clay said he had an appointment to keep, but Chuck clutched the back of his shoulder and shoved him down the street. Soon they were at a local joint and Chuck was ordering Depth Charges: a glass of beer and shot of whiskey. While Clay sipped the beer and ignored the whiskey, Chuck ignored the beer and threw back the whiskey. "I really shouldn't drink when I'm working." Chuck held up his shot glass to let the bartender know he was ready for another.

"Maybe I should let you get back to the office."

"You think I work in some office pushing paper? I'm working right now."

"What's your line?"

"I'm a private eye. That should come as no big surprise. Remember all those stories we used to read in your bedroom? Besides, I figured I'd put that military training to good use."

"You're serious, you're a private detective?"

"I guess it's what I always wanted. Too bad it's not quite so exciting as I figured. Or important. But then what is, compared to a world war? And even that was a disappointment."

"What do you mean?"

"It was just a colossal mess. Whole countries slaughtering each other. And for what? So we can do it all over again in a few years?" Chuck began waving his shot glass in the air, calling for another. "Maybe you had the right idea all along. Maybe I should have been a conscientious objector."

"The only thing I objected to was doing what my parents wanted."

"Sorry to hear about their passing."

"What are you talking about?"

"You didn't hear?"

"Hear what?"

"Oh man, they're dead. The both of them. You didn't know?"

Clay reached out for his own shot of whiskey and threw it back. They sat quietly for a minute before Clay asked, "How did it happen?"

"Your mom got cancer. And after she passed, I guess he didn't feel like living. It happens. You just lose the desire. Trust me, I've seen it. But I really don't know what the doctors called it."

Clay now held up his glass to get the attention of the bartender. "What about your folks?"

"What about them? They moved to Ohio. We have family there. Nothing like family to sell worthless shit to. I guess we drifted apart."

"What's it matter? We're here. They're not. So what are you working on right now? Anything exciting?"

"The usual divorce work. Some broad's attorney is paying me to get the goods on her old man. The hours are irregular, but it pays the bills and I'm my own boss. What did you say your line is, Clay?"

"I don't have a line. I don't even have a job right now."

"Come work for me, then."

"Are you crazy?"

"I'm serious, pal. I actually have an office, but I've gone through a dozen secretaries. I need more of an associate, not someone to just answer the phone and type up a letter. I need to expand the business. I need somebody to field inquiries who can think, who can fill in for me if needed."

"Fill in for you? Chuck, you're Goddamn imposing. Look at me. Who's going to take me seriously?"

"Ah, it's all an act. You dress up a mobster like a soda jerk and the guy doesn't exactly strike terror in your heart. But you put a suit on a soda jerk and crease his fedora just so, and you piss your pants if he looks your way. Just an act. I'll show you the ropes. You'll do fine."

"I don't know."

"You're hired. Just one thing."

"What's that?"

"No drinking on the job."

The next day, Clay started his new job as an associate of a private operative. Chuck had rented a suite of offices at the end of the top floor of a Center City office building, right next to a janitor's closet and the stairs. All day, Clay would hear mop buckets being filled and emptied and the footsteps of people marching between floors rather than wait for the building's rickety elevator. Beyond the frosted-glass front door, the suite consisted of a small outer office with a desk, filing cabinet, a fat Royal typewriter perched on a metal stand, and a pair of side chairs. Chuck's inner office was larger and included a sink and mirror in the corner. A john was located down the hall, next to a dentist's office that never seemed to have any patients.

In one corner of Clay's desk was an in-box that doubled as an out-box and a place for Chuck's odd change. There was also a blotter and a squat black Ma Bell telephone, the kind that was heavy enough to bludgeon someone to death, provided the cord reached. In the front drawer of the desk, Clay found pencil nubs, assorted paperclips, and bullets of two different calibers, .38s and .45s. He also found several coffee-stained business cards. Charles Lefebvre & Associates, Discreet Inquiries.

On his first morning as Chuck's associate, Clay straightened up the office, which took about five minutes, and waited for the phone to ring or for a mysterious figure to rap on the frosted glass. The only call was a wrong number, and the only person to pass through the door was Chuck, who arrived shortly before noon.

"The mail come yet?"

"Nope."

"If there's a check inside, keep it. If it's a bill, toss it. Any calls?"

"Nope."

"Good."

"Isn't that bad? For business, I mean."

"I'm all booked up, anyway. I'm going to take a nap. Wake me up in an hour."

"I guess you can't be that booked up."

"Clay, here's the scoop. I work mostly at night. Private ops are like vampires. That's when we come alive. That's when I follow husbands on the loose. Pass on envelopes and pretend like I don't know there's cash inside. Sometimes I visit guys to remind them a payment is past due. When you're roused out of bed at three in the morning with a rod in your face, you tend to be more receptive to reason. The early morning is also a good time to pay a call to after-hours drinking holes to drum up new business. But I still need to have an office and spend some time here. Maybe someone will want to call to check up on me. Maybe they're especially industrious and they walk all the way the fuck up here to make sure the address on my card isn't to some dentist office. By the way, the dentist office next to the men's room, it's not a dentist office."

"What is it?"

"The guy does abortions at night. He's also one of our clients. Once every two weeks I deliver his payoff to the local precinct captain through a cutout. I'm not supposed to know who's getting the dough, but the cutout is an old buddy of mine from the service in the same line of work. We're a small fraternity of fixers with our own code. We never screw each other unless we can get away with it. The only fiduciary responsibility you have is to yourself. Remember that."

"Aren't you supposed to do what's right for your client?"

"The kind of people we represent assume we're looking out for ourselves. If they don't think you're looking out for yourself, they don't figure you're the kind of guy who can fix their problems. They're not asking you to repair their Goddamn car. They need someone who knows what to do without being told exactly what to do. They don't really want to know what you do. They just want to know that what needs to get done gets done. That means they know they're dealing with basically unscrupulous people, guys who are going to look after themselves and likely take a cut off the top or play something to their own advantage. That's all factored into it. That's why they trust guys like me."

"Because they can't trust you?"

"Exactly. And that concludes your first lesson of the trade. Don't trust anyone you can trust."

"I don't know if I'm cut out for this, Chuck."

"Sure you are. You're a born liar."

"I'm not very tough."

"Yeah, but we mostly don't deal with tough guys. We deal with guys who have less grit than a poodle in a skirt. We'll get you some new cheap suits. They're expensive but worth it."

"Cheap suits are expensive?"

"You can't wear just any cheap suit. And you need to start carrying a gun. We'll get you a permit if it makes you feel better."

"I can't carry a gun."

"They're not that heavy."

"What if I have to use it? I can't shoot anybody."

"Sure, you can. Anybody can. That's generally the problem."

"I don't want to carry a gun."

"Some guys get away with it. But you have to talk tougher. Clay, you need to carry a gun. The weight under your armpit inspires the tough talk."

"I don't know."

"It's just a tool. Like a saw. You give a guy a saw and pretty soon he starts acting like a carpenter. Carry a gun, Clay. You'll see what I mean." Chuck flipped open his jacket and pulled a snub-nosed .38 from a leather holster under his arm. He pulled a pin below the barrel to crack open the chamber, emptied the bullets into the in-box on Clay's desk, slapped the chamber back in place, and placed the gun on the blotter. "Get the feel of it. I'm taking a nap."

28

"Clay, talk to me." Ryan clutched Clay by the shoulder and pushed him back into the chair until he looked at him. "Did you shoot Barrett?"

"Who?"

"Never mind. The police won't get anything out of him. He doesn't know what's going on."

"Maybe we can keep this quiet?" Phyllis said.

"You really think so? In this day and age? You can't keep anything a secret."

Phyllis turned to Vivian. "We need to reach a settlement between us before this all gets out."

"It was the kid's fault," Clay said, but everyone ignored him. Maybe everything else in his life was confusing, but Clay knew what they were talking about when it came to HCA. Clay had recited the whole story to his neurologist, telling him how the Pembroke kid talked Vivian into changing lawyers. So, you see, it was all the kid's fault.

"The new hotshot lawyers rejected the $5 million offer on the table and made a counteroffer of $50 million. Ryan didn't even bother to sweeten his bid. The two sides were just too far apart."

"How's your appetite been?" his doctor asked.

"The problem was that the arbitrator had already made his decision, and so all Ryan had to do was send the check for the $4.5 million valuation. If Vivian wanted the $5 million courtesy amount, she had 48 hours to change her mind."

"Mr. White, did you have breakfast this morning?"

"Of course, I had breakfast this morning."

"What did you have?"

"I had breakfast for breakfast, what the fuck do you think I had? Lunch?"

Rather than tell his neurologist what he ate, Clay patiently explained that his granddaughter's new lawyers filed a law suit, asking the court to void the stock agreement between Steve and Ryan. The arbitrator and company accountants were slammed in the petition, a conspiracy was hinted at, and the buy-sell agreement was portrayed as a shameful attempt to take advantage of an inexperienced young man who was still suffering from the loss of his parents in a horrendous automobile accident.

"That's absolutely fascinating," the neurologist said. "Maybe you can tell me more in, say, a month."

That night, Clay was watching the Phillies game at Vivian's home when Pembroke showed up unannounced to talk about the matter, but Clay was all talked out. He just wanted to watch the game and was having enough trouble following that.

"Maybe I should just take the offer," Vivian said.

"They're bluffing."

"What if they're not? Maybe my original lawyers were right. They said if I went to court, the legal fees would eat up as much and maybe more than whatever extra money I could get out of the deal."

"You have to hang tough. They're overplaying their hand. They're more desperate than they look."

"I don't need the stress. And for what? Money? There's more important things than money."

"Only people who have money ever say that. If you don't have money, it's the only thing that matters. I know."

"That's the point. I have enough money."

"Not enough. Not nearly enough."

"Enough for what? Tell me, Tom. Enough for what?"

Pembroke reached out for Vivian's hand. "It's not enough . . . for us."

Vivian pulled her hand away, stood behind Clay and began messaging his shoulders.

"Is the game over? Who won?" Clay asked.

"Come on, you know how I feel about you," Tom told her. "How I've always felt about you." Pembroke reached out and petted Clay's gray head.

"If I ever gave you the impression that I had any feeling for you other than friendship—"

"Come on, Vivian, you know that's not true. Don't act like you didn't know I was . . . interested. From the time I saw you at the Phillies game with your grandfather when you first came back to town. You knew. Women always know."

"I'm talking about now. Since I got married."

"With all due respect, Steve didn't treat you right. I can understand why you would want him . . . dealt with."

"What?"

"What do the politicians call it? Plausible deniability? You drop hints that if something should happen to your cheating cad of a husband, that wouldn't be the worst thing in the world as far as you're concerned."

"What are you talking about, Tom?"

"You know what I'm talking about. Phyllis told me what you really wanted done. She knows everything."

"I think it's time for you to go."

"Come on, Vivian."

"I want you to leave!"

"So that's how it is? You don't need anyone now?"

"Just leave. I'll try to forget you ever suggested what I think you're suggesting."

"This is all a show, isn't it? Fine. Whatever. If that's what you need to work through the guilt of everything."

"Just go."

"Sure, I'll go." Pembroke patted Clay on the head.

The next day, Vivian called her attorneys, but before she had a chance to tell them to accept Ryan's $5 million offer, she learned the game had changed. Steve's brother Barrett had just arrived in Philly with a copy of Steve's will.

"What's the will say?" Clay asked.

"Barrett gets almost everything."

What Barrett actually possessed was a copy of Steve's will. His lawyer went to court asking that it be recognized, suggesting that the original must have been destroyed or hidden by unnamed parties who stood to benefit from the lack of a will. Ryan's offer to Vivian was rescinded, and Ryan sided with Barrett regarding the validity of the will in his possession. Ryan's side offered Barrett $2 million for his HCA stock. Barrett's lawyer said that nothing less than $75 million would satisfy his client. Talks soon broke off, and two days later Ryan's lawyer went to court to share a new revelation.

"Grandpa, you'll never guess what happened."

"Tell me."

"Ryan and Phyllis found a will that predates Barrett's will. And it's signed."

"It's a forgery!"

"I saw it. It looks good to me."

In the new will, Steve Hess declared that because of his decades of loyal service to HCA, Ryan would receive all but a token amount of his stock in the company, essentially leaving Vivian and Barrett out of the picture. Barrett's lawyers then said they discovered yet another will. Not only was it the latest one yet, it was a signed original and came with an affidavit from a handwriting expert stating that the signature was without doubt that of the late Steve Hess.

"Now he says he wants $100 million for the stock he's going to inherit," Vivian told Clay over breakfast.

Clay was listening, but he was also trying to etch in his mind what he was eating, getting ready for his appointment with the doctor that morning.

* * *

Apparently everyone in the hotel room was talking about Clay. They were certainly looking at him.

"He's just not all there," Ryan said.

"You really think he did it?" Vivian asked.

"Of course he did it!" Phyllis threw her hands in the air, looking like an ump calling a foul ball. "His fingerprints are probably all over the gun."

"He might have just picked it up. He was looking at it when I walked in. That doesn't mean he used it."

"A gun in his hand, a dead body on the floor, come on, honey. Face the facts."

"Stranger things have happened," Ryan said. "Just when you think you've seen it all."

"Are you still a private snoop?" Clay asked.

"No, I gave that up a long time ago," Ryan said

"Miss it?"

"No, not really. It was a tedious life. A lot of waiting around and trying to look tough."

Look tough. That was what Chuck had always preached. Whether it was the West Coast or the East, the game was the same. It was Chuck who took Clay to a haberdashery where he bought him a pair of suits and a new hat. So he could look tough. Clay wore one of the suits out of the store. Their next stop was a pawn shop where Clay was outfitted with his own Smith & Wesson .38 and holster. He wore this out of the store as well, although unloaded. Chuck promised to take Clay out to the woods someday for target practice. "For now," Chuck said, "just get used to the weight and feel of a cannon under your arm. Feels good, huh?"

"Uncomfortable is more like it."

Their next stop was Arch Street on the edge of Chinatown and the law office of a man named Leonard Pell. At least, that was the name listed on the shingle that hung by a flight of wooden stairs that led to the guy's walkup at the bookend of a row house block. They found Pell sitting at a cluttered desk gluing the sole of his shoe. Pell was small, gaunt, gray haired, and yellow-skinned. He glanced up from his task and asked, "Who's this?"

"My new associate, Miles Archer."

"That's your tough luck, Miles. Nice suit. It's over there."

Pell nodded toward a case of frayed law books by the door. On top was a fat yellow unmarked envelope. Chuck stuffed it into an inner pocket of his jacket, tipped his hat, and they left Pell to repair his shoe.

As they descended the stairs, Clay asked, "Why'd you call me Miles Archer?"

"It's a joke."

"I don't think he got it."

"I did."

In their car, Chuck removed the envelope to inspect it. He told Clay that he was supposed to deliver it to another operative who would pass it on to somebody else who would pass it along to yet another cutout.

"What's the point?" Clay asked.

"Well by the time this reaches its last stop it's passed through so many hands, no one would know where the chain began. The only thing you know is who gave it to you and who you gave it to."

Chuck pinched the envelope with both hands, starting from the edge and working his way to the middle. "There's some smaller envelopes inside this one."

"Are you supposed to be doing that?"

"Here's another lesson of the trade. Knowledge is power. It's always good to have something to hold over somebody else because you have to assume they have something they can hold over you. It feels like a key."

Chuck handed the envelop to Clay who fingered it. "I guess so. But it's kind of small."

"I'd say it either fits a bus locker or a safety deposit box. Oh well, let's go make the drop off at Palumbo's and get something to eat."

The main room at Palumbo's was half empty when Chuck and Clay arrived, the first floor show of the evening still two hours away. Chuck spotted his man at the bar. Standing six-seven, he was hard to miss.

"Sparrow, I want you to meet my new associate, Miles Archer."

Sparrow shook Clay's hand. "Pleasure, Miles. Chuck and me work plenty together."

"We make beautiful music."

They had a couple of drinks with Sparrow, and at some point, Chuck laid an envelope on the bar, Sparrow picked it up, and stashed it inside his jacket. A few minutes later they left Sparrow at the bar and sat at a table to have dinner.

While they ate, every few moments someone Chuck knew would stop by to say hello. Each time, Chuck introduced Clay as Miles Archer, even though nobody got the joke.

29

Bettendorf. Focus. Barrett. She's your granddaughter. Vivian. Focus. Clay leafed through sticky notes on the chair arm while people kept talking in the room. How was he supposed to focus with all that chatter? Bettendorf. Barrett. Box top. Clay peeled off the last note. Box top? Was that supposed to mean something?

Clay reached into his jacket pocket and found... nothing. Was he expecting to find a box top? He searched his other pocket, suddenly desperate to find the box top. If he didn't find the box top, how was he going to recognize his contact? But, of course, it wasn't a box top he was missing, it was half of a box top. Whoever he was supposed to meet held the other half. That was the point, to bring two strangers together. One with the assignment, and the other meant to carry it out.

"The team looks good this year," Clay whispered to himself. "They're just a bunch of bums."

Hadn't Clay already met the man with the matching half of the box top? That's why there was no box top.

And then what? He was supposed to do something. What was it? Was he late doing it? And what about the dry cleaning? Clay noticed more notes stuck to the side of the chair, and in a panic he pulled them off, one by one, desperate to learn where he was supposed to be. Southwark. Ellis. Snake Alley. J.

Who was J? A face came to mind. A comma of black hair on a forehead. Wire-rim glasses. A sparse mustache. A startled look when Clay pointed a gun in his face. Yes, he remembered J. He remembered forcing the guy back inside the machine shop he owned and was about to close up for the night.

"There's no cash. My partner already took it to the bank." This J was scared. A poodle in a skirt.

Clay closed the door and latched it behind his back. "I don't want anything, Julius."

"How do you know my name?"

"We have friends in common."

"Who?"

"Do you really need to ask?"

"I've been trying for years to make contact, and now you show up. There's nothing I can do. It's too dangerous. Don't you read the newspapers?"

"You're lucky I do read them. I should have just done the job and not thought about it."

"You mean, they want to... After the service I've given?"

"You can never give them enough service. They're not who you think they are. And you're not who you think you are. What, you should be treated like a hero? You know what you are, Julius Rosenberg? You're a loose end. You know things you shouldn't know."

"I'll keep my mouth shut."

"You'll talk. David's probably talking already."

"I told him to leave the country after Gold got arrested. He didn't listen."

"How much you want to bet him and his wife are selling you out right now? Then you'll start talking, and you know how our friends like to keep secrets almost as much as they like to steal them."

"So that's it, you've come to murder me? To keep me quiet?"

"That was the picture, but maybe the picture's changed."

"How? You want money? I don't have much. Maybe I could try to raise some."

"I don't want your dough. I don't want anything from you. I'm just telling you what's what. The thing is, you're a believer. I never was. I've been a prisoner all my life, but now I'm going to set myself free. I have my own business to attend to. I have my own life. And I just wanted to tell somebody I fucking quit. And who better than you?"

"So you're not going to... "

"No. I just dropped in to say hello and goodbye." Clay slipped his pistol in the pocket of his raincoat, turned to open the door, and a moment later was on the sidewalk blending into the crowd on Houston Street.

Clay stared at the letter J written on a Post-It note. So there was no place he needed to be. He had already not done what he was supposed to do.

Why were they all yammering in the room? He looked up to see Ryan talking to...was that Lynne? What were they talking about? The fire in the boat house? She had been pretty shook up. Clay remembered checking up on her later that night.

It was Ryan who had answered the door.

"I heard you've volunteered to be the kid's guardian angel." Ryan held a newspaper in his one good hand, reading glasses perched on his forehead.

"Is she still up?"

"Her husband called. Remember him? You want to drive her home and leave me to my paper?"

"Did you catch the game tonight?"

"The Phils win?"

"Lost. Again."

"They stink."

Clay agreed to give Lynne a lift. She was wearing one of Phyllis's dresses. A loose white chemise that could be made to fit with a belt. She offered Clay a weak smile as she descended the stairs. She said she was ready to go, pecked Phyllis on the cheek at the door, and said goodbye to Ryan who had returned to reading his paper in the living room. Clay led Lynne to his car parked down the street and opened the door for her. He circled around and as soon he pulled himself behind the steering wheel, Lynne clutched his hand, lay her head against his shoulder, and curled her legs on the seat.

"You doing okay?" Clay asked.

"Yes. Not really. Better, now that you're here, darling."

"You should probably hold the sweet talk, Mrs. Stoller."

"I don't want to go home. I'm tired of making up lies for him."

"You want me to tell him the truth?"

"No."

"I'm going to have to tell him something. As far as he knows I just met you. Kind of odd I just happen to be the one driving you home."

"Drop me off at a cab stand. There's one a few blocks from the house. Phyllis won't say anything."

"You're good."

"We both know that's not true." Clay started the car and put it in gear to pull away. "I hate myself sometimes."

"Really?"

"But I hate him more. I can't take it anymore, Clay. You don't know what it's like."

"I can see where this is going."

"If that was him in the boat house, I'd be dead. He might find a way to get himself out, but he'd leave me behind. You didn't. And more than that . . . you love me. Or you could love me. And I could love you."

"If only we could be together, anything's possible. Just you and me and your mister's money."

"Do you know what it feels like to be trapped? To be living a life you didn't really choose? To wish you could just change your name and go somewhere and start all over?"

"What makes you think I don't?"

"Well, you can't do that without money. Without money you stay trapped."

"And here I thought money was the root of all evil."

"That's what they want you to think, the people with all the money who don't want to give it up. You know what money is? Freedom. Freedom to be who you want, where you want."

"You need to go home and get some sleep."

"Still, wouldn't it be nice to just start all over?"

Clay dropped off Lynne at the cab stand, gave her a few dollars, and left her to find the rest of the way home. He then drove back to her step-parents' place. He could see Ryan in the living room, still finding something worth reading in the evening *Bulletin*. Now Clay tapped his horn and kept tapping it until Ryan turned to look out the window. Clay flashed his high beams twice. Ryan took off his reading glasses and came to the window. Clay tapped the horn and flashed his lights at the same time.

Ryan disappeared from the window for a moment, the front door opened, and he walked down the path in his slippers to Clay's car. Ryan opened the car door and looked in to find Clay pointing a pistol at his belly and telling him to get in the car.

"What's this all about?"

"Just get in." As soon as Ryan took a seat and closed the door, Clay drove up the block while keeping the gun trained on Ryan, pulled over, and killed the lights.

"Now what?" Ryan looked more curious than scared.

"It's all been you."

"It's all been me, what?"

"I'm not saying there aren't any unanswered questions. There are plenty. You didn't kill Ellis. I saw who did. And you didn't try to bump off me and Lynne."

"I thought you two got caught in the rain or jumped in a pool or something. Jesus, if I had known

I would have put my paper down. What else is on the scorecard?"

"Bettendorf."

"You need to go home and get some rest, Clay."

"Bettendorf."

"I'm guessing that's supposed to mean something to me."

"It's Stoller's little secret. The one you're blackmailing him about."

"You know, Clay, you're lucky I used to be in the business. I know how an op wants to feel like what he does is more important than what it is. There's always some big secret hiding around the corner, and if you look hard enough, take all the punches, bend all the rules, you'll find it. And whatever it is will make up for whatever you need to make up for in your crappy life. Only it never does."

"You found out about Bettendorf and you sent Stoller those blackmail notes. You had it in for the guy. The way I see it, you don't like being the one-armed muscleman for a stocking company. You want to be a partner, only your buddy Hess isn't so accommodating. But he needs money to expand and if you come up with the dough to help build that new plant, you get a stake in the business. You get to make up for whatever it is you need to make up for in your crappy little life."

"That's what you think?"

"You don't have that kind of dough, but you know someone who does. Our pal Stoller. Married to your kid. You ask for a loan. He says, 'Sure thing.' We're all family, right? But this is business, and when it comes to business, Stoller doesn't give a shit about family. Hess wants money to buy land to build a plant, but why lend you the money to buy into this little sweetheart of a business when Stoller can just trade a property he has in South Philly, get a piece of the company for himself, and save his dough? Of course that means you get cut out of the deal."

"I'll give you that much, op. He did cut me out."

"And you weren't happy about it."

"No, I was not."

"So you started to dig. There's always something people have to hide, and Stoller was more likely than most to have a big skeleton in the closet."

"Bettendorf."

"That's right. Bettendorf. You start your letter writing campaign. It's a two-prong attack. You've got to stop that plant from being built, so you send letters to Hess warning him to stay out of The Neck. But he doesn't scare, so you try to make problems with the site through the housing inspector. Only he's already on the take, so he's too afraid to interfere. But he's got a brother, Inspector Craig Ellis, who has something in his past you work up. And the timing is perfect, what with the sitting of the Grand Jury and the Senate committee in town. You send Ellis a few little blue notes to get him to put pressure on his brother to stop the new plant from going up."

"And then I kill him for some reason."

"No, sometimes shit just happens. But good for you, the job shuts down. Now if only you can raise some funds to buy into HCA."

"Bettendorf."

"Like I said, a two-prong attack. And that was a clever piece of business, sending a blackmail note to your wife. Anything you paid would just be going back to yourself."

"I suppose it's gratifying to finally have my work appreciated."

"So you don't deny it?"

"Clay, I actually do like you. I'd love to make you feel good and make a play for the gun or try to run away. You know, some way to admit my guilt. The only problem is, you got the wrong guy. I don't know what in the world Bettendorf means. What I do know is I haven't been blackmailing Stoller or my own company. Sure, I'd like to be a part-owner of HCA. But it doesn't mean that much to me. I'm not that ambitious. Hell, ask my wife."

Clay raised the revolver and pointed it between Ryan's eyes.

"It's past my bedtime," Ryan said. "I'm ready to go to sleep one way or the other."

Twenty seconds later, Clay finally lowered the gun.

"You're in a 'me-first' business," Ryan said. "I know. I've been there. In every case there's only one mystery that needs to be solved . . . What's in it for me? Everything else is whipped cream. Who cares who's blackmailing who? What's the payoff for yours truly? What do you get from figuring it out? Is it less than what you'd get for not figuring it out? What's in it for you? That's the only question that ever matters in your line of work."

Ryan opened the door, slipped out of the car, and made his way back to his house.

251

30

Everything was so muddled. Clay wasn't even sure who he was anymore. But maybe that wasn't so odd. Hadn't there been a time when as far as the world was concerned there was no Clay White? There was just Miles Archer. All of Chuck's circle of friends, operatives, informers, and assorted ne'er-do-well acquaintances knew him as Miles. Clay had not bothered to correct Chuck in the beginning and soon it became too much trouble to try to set the record straight. Eventually, even Chuck dropped the occasional use of his real name. Miles it was, and Clay decided to just accept it. Perhaps it was just as well. Life as Clay White, conscientious objector was no peach. Miles Archer, associate to a private investigator, held more promise.

He was an associate in name only, of course. Chuck never made the time to take Clay to the woods to learn how to shoot his .38, and Clay fell out of the habit of strapping the holster to his side and sliding the gun in place when he went out. Eventually the gun and holster found a permanent place in one of his desk drawers at the office. And it wasn't like Clay did any work for Chuck outside of the office. He was really more Chuck's secretary and nag than he was his associate. He should have been called Miss Wonderly. There was certainly no danger of getting bumped off by Bridget or Thursby or whoever the hell it was that shot his namesake.

Clay needed to be a nag because Chuck began to drink more and tend to business less. Chuck had been melancholy ever since they had become reacquainted, but his mood grew decidedly more sullen after one of his Army buddies passed away. The guy had suffered for years, paralyzed and barely conscious, a vegetable in a hospital bed. He finally died officially, and when Chuck returned from the funeral he retreated to his office with a bottle, locked the door, and didn't come out until the next day, pissing in the sink when he had to. Chuck went back to work, fixing the problems of others, but whatever enjoyment he took in being an operative had long passed. He began turning down work and drinking more than ever. After a couple of weeks, the inquiries Clay fielded became less frequent as old clients turned to other, more reliable sources of assistance.

Chuck began arriving at the office later in the day and leaving sooner, and always drunk. Chuck was not a fall-down foolish drunk, just quiet and dark. Not yet thirty and he looked like he was forty and heading for fifty. Without fail, Clay came to the office each day despite the lack of anything to do. Not only had he reorganized the files, he read every one out of boredom. They contained notes typed up by himself and his predecessors. It was far from the stuff of pulp fiction.

4:00 A.M. Arrived at Maywood Drive. Subject left home at 7:30. Followed to Lincoln Diner, 8:00. And on and on in monotonous detail.

Finally, Clay started to write letters to his father again. He knew the man was dead and would never read them, but it passed the time. More than that, it kept Clay White alive, kept him from completely becoming Miles Archer, the ultimate bit player. Clay wrote about meeting Chuck again and learning the detective business. How to talk. How to wear a cheap suit and where to buy one. And when he ran out of things to write about Chuck, Clay recalled the past, still wondering how things went wrong in his family.

One afternoon while Clay was writing a letter, Chuck arrived at the office carrying a captain's wheel clock missing the minute hand. He placed it on Clay's desk, and said, "Here."

"You want me to have it fixed?"

"No, it's yours. I want you to have it."

"It's broken."

"It works. It's just missing a hand. You get used to it."

The next day, Chuck presented Clay with half a dictionary. The following day it was a pen knife missing one of its blades. Over the next two weeks Chuck came into the office infrequently but when he did, he brought a gift for Clay, who listed them all in the letters he wrote to his dead father. Chuck gave him one half of a pair of shoes, a belt with no buckle, a table radio missing the cord, a canteen without a cap, and a stool with only two-thirds of its legs. Eventually, Chuck came in one afternoon, opened his jacket, and removed the .38 from his holster.

"What are you writing?" Chuck said. "I didn't know we had any business anymore."

"It's a letter. To my father."

"I told you, he's dead."

"I know."

"Okay." Chuck laid the .38 on the desk blotter next to Clay's sheet of stationery. "I want you to have this."

Don't you need it?"

"I'm taking a trip." Chuck removed his jacket.

"Where?"

"I don't know. Wherever the train stops." He unbuckled his holster and laid it next to the gun. "I want you to have this, too."

"Chuck, are you okay?"

"I'm fine."

"When are you coming back?"

"I'm not."

"What?"

"The business is all yours, Miles, if you want it. The super will put your name on the door. Just tell him."

"You're just going who knows where? What are you going to do?"

"Probably drink myself to death. Who knows, maybe I'll get creative. Go back to your letter. Tell The Rev I said hi."

Chuck slipped on his jacket and left the office. The next day when he failed to show up, Clay called his apartment. There was no answer. The following day after Chuck again failed to come into the office, Clay visited his apartment. When no one answered, Clay told the landlord he was worried about his friend. They entered and found the place empty, albeit littered with spent whiskey bottles and overtaxed ash trays.

Two weeks passed and still no sign of Chuck. Clay remained hopeful that he would soon show up tanned and rested, but after a month he lost hope. The rent was due and there was still money in the business account, so Clay paid the bills and kept coming into the office, kept writing letters he would never send. Occasionally someone called, looking for an operative, and Clay would say Chuck was overbooked at the moment but might be available in a week or so.

When Clay wasn't writing, he read the newspapers, mostly scanning the want ads. As Clay eventually lost heart over Chuck's return, it became a true job search. When the money in the business checking account ran out, Clay called to have the telephone removed. Once the phone was gone, he planned to give notice to the landlord and begin applying for one of those jobs he had circled in the newspapers.

Clay was circling a want ad in the *Inquirer* when he heard a rap on the frosted glass door. Without looking up, he called out, "Come in." Assuming that the person entering the office was from Ma Bell to come fetch the phone, he said, "Am I in your way?"

"I didn't expect to find you here, Clay."

Clay couldn't remember the last time he had heard his real name. He looked up. The man in the dark suit that stood before him looked vaguely familiar.

"Don't you remember me? It's Johnny."

"Johnny?"

"Johnny LeMaster. Back from the dead."

* * *

Clay heard someone say, "I found something." A moment later, Ryan returned to the room. "Looks like a homemade silencer." Ryan held up a two-liter soda bottle stuffed with charred ceiling insulation and an opening cut out for the gun barrel.

"Will that work?" asked a young woman who could have been either Clay's wife or his granddaughter.

"Good enough so that the neighbors won't take notice and you could leave without drawing any attention," Ryan said.

Phyllis turned to Clay. "So why didn't you leave?"

"Are you talking to me?" Clay couldn't understand why everyone was staring at him. He began looking through his notes. Snake Alley. Box Top. Barrett. Clay had a feeling this had to do with Barrett.

"I don't even know why I'm trying to get through to him. He made that silencer thing and shot Barrett. End of story."

"Is he even capable of making it?" Vivian asked. "How did he even know I was going to be here? For that matter, Phyllis, how did you and your husband know I was here?"

"We make a point of keeping tabs on things."

"You mean you've been spying on me?"

"Our lawyers have people who work for them," Ryan said.

"Private eyes, you mean. Paid to spy on me."

"Yes. It's regrettable. But that's the situation we find ourselves in."

"This is important to everyone," Phyllis said. "We just want to do what's fair for everyone."

"Only there's one less party to deal with. Isn't that convenient?"

"Are you suggesting something?"

"Like what did you have in mind?"

"We certainly didn't arrange his murder. Barrett was a disagreeable young man. He always was. I'm not afraid to admit I never cared for him. And I would have been glad to see him leave and never come back. But I never wished him harm."

"It's just money," Ryan said.

"People kill for money all the time," Vivian answered.

"Sometimes, but not always. Most times, people kill because they're afraid or they're angry. Most times, people kill the people they love."

"Most times, people don't come prepared with homemade silencers."

"True. This isn't most times."

"We only came here tonight to see if we could work out something without the lawyers causing a fuss," Phyllis said.

"That's what I was trying to do," Vivian said.

"But without us. You were going to join forces with Barrett."

"I didn't trust him any more than you did. I'm sick of this whole thing. He could have all of the stock in the company. That's what I came to tell him. I want to be done with it. I hate that company. All I want is the house, the cars, the money Steve and I had in the bank, and any other outside investments. You guys can fight over the company and what it's worth."

"But now Barrett's gone, no matter who's to blame. What do you plan to do with the company now?"

"Phyllis, there's been a murder! Who cares about that at the moment? I'm worried that my grandfather is about to be arrested."

"Of course, you're right. Another time, another place."

"They both did it," Clay said

"Who did what?" asked Vivian.

"They both killed him."

"There were two people who did the shooting? Are you sure?"

"They didn't shoot him. They made it look like an accident. Crushed his skull."

"Who are you talking about?"

"Clearly he's not referring to Barrett," Phyllis began walking to the kitchen. "Probably mixing up reality with one of his cheap detective novels filled with outlandish coincidences and the sudden appearance of sordid characters."

There was a fresh knock at the door. Phyllis was the closest and checked the peephole to see who it might be. "Oh my God," she said. "What's he doing here?"

31

The man in the hallway was Tom Pembroke. Phyllis informed him through the closed door that it would be best that he went away.

"Forget it. I'm not going anywhere."

"Let him in," Vivian said. "He wants to become involved so much, let him. He'll get to deal with the police, too."

"It's already a bit crowded." Phyllis rested her hand on the knob as Pembroke began to hammer on the door again. She finally relented and turned the latch. Once inside, Pembroke was given the tour. The dead body, the murder weapon, the homemade silencer.

All of this over HCA. Years ago. And again today.

Clay knew that most of the recent fight over HCA had been fought in the newspapers and on television. His granddaughter kept him well informed. Maybe Clay didn't remember what he did five minutes earlier but he knew Ryan's side rejected Barrett's $100 million price for his HCA stock, insisting that if the company was liquidated it would only fetch a fraction of that amount. Instead, Ryan's lawyers promised to contest the validity of the latest incarnation of Steve's will in court. Everything about the will, his lawyers said, was dubious, not just the signature. The brothers had never been close. Both had, in fact, expressed their disdain for one another on numerous occasions. What evidence was there that Steve would write a will that almost exclusively redounded to the benefit of his black sheep brother? Barrett's lawyers responded by leaking to the *Inquirer* the news that they had a witness to the signing of the will, someone who felt compelled by a sense of justice to come forward, someone who happened to be present when the two brothers were reunited, hugged, wept, reminisced about their parents, and discussed the idea of writing wills that named each other as the primary beneficiary. On the courthouse steps, Barrett's lawyer held up for the sake of the cameras a copy of Barrett's will that left everything to his brother. Not said was what Barrett might own that was worth leaving to his brother. Nevertheless, Barrett's mystery witness had seen the documents signed. That was the important point. The press implored Barrett's lawyer to provide a name. At first it appeared that no name would be forthcoming. Surely, he said, no one would question the word of the man who was willing to testify under oath that he heard the wills discussed and witnessed the signing of the document outlining Steve's last wishes. Then the lawyer thrilled the pack by revealing that his witness was Steve Hess' closest friend, the best man at his wedding, a member of one of the Main Line's oldest and most respected families. Did anyone seriously doubt the word of Tom Pembroke?

"I told you not to trust the kid," Clay told his granddaughter. "It's all his fault."

The momentum of the case, at least in the eyes of the Philadelphia media, had swung in Barrett's direction. It didn't take too much digging by Ryan's side, however, to find that in the years since he and his parents severed ties, Barrett had been involved in several scrapes with the law and barely avoided prosecution. There was the older gentleman from Boca Raton who befriended Barrett only to discovered that some jewelry went missing. Barrett, who insisted the jewelry was a present, was held for questioning, but the matter was quickly dropped when the older gentleman decided that he'd rather not explain why he had taken Barrett with him on a vacation to St. Croix and a skiing trip to Vail and a shopping spree on Rodeo Drive. Then there was the matter with the lottery ticket. Barrett sold it to a man, telling him that he couldn't cash it or his ex-wife would have the money seized for back child support payments. The lottery ticket was legitimate, but the story Barrett told and the newspaper clipping he used to support it were fake. The frustrated ticket holder went to the police, but there was no hard evidence to back his claim, and no charges were filed.

"And then there's the misdemeanor charges," Vivian told Clay. "Drug possession, trespassing, solicitation. Ryan's lawyers say they painted a picture of a serial opportunist."

"What's Barrett's lawyer say?"

"That it's just a ham-fisted attempt to smear a fine young man who's trying to deal with the loss of his brother. All they say that matters is Tom's integrity, the witness to the will. Obviously they don't know Tom."

That's when hints were leaked to the press that Pembroke was beginning to question whether he had actually witnessed Steve signing a will or a contract for something entirely unrelated. And there was a good chance, now that Tom had some time to think about it, that Barrett had come to Philadelphia that last time to extract a few more dollars out of his kid brother. Ryan's side was now deemed the frontrunner by seasoned court observers.

And now what did it matter? Barrett was dead. Clay looked at the note with "Barrett" written on it. Barrett wasn't just dead. He had been murdered. Solving the murder was the problem at hand. Not what happened decades ago. Clay had to focus on the here and now. But he couldn't. Vivid memories pressed in, memories that demanded an audience. No matter how intently he stared at the note, Clay thought about another time, another place. He thought about a train. A train he took to New York one Sunday morning.

After arriving at Penn Station, Clay took the subway to Brooklyn, getting out at the Prospect Park station. From there he just followed the crowd past the Botanical Gardens. Soon he could see Ebbets Field. The day before, the Dodgers and Phillies had attracted less than capacity, about 24,000, but today was different. Today the locals were convinced that the Dodgers would actually catch up to the Phillies in the standings and force a playoff. Every ticket was sold, but if you were willing to pay a premium, a ticket could be had from the smart-talking speculators who always seemed to have a ready supply of seats. Clay settled for the upper deck of left field. Ebbets was a lot like Shibe Park in Philly. Both had been shoehorned into a city block, and neither had enough room in right field for bleachers. Because of the dimensions, the Dodgers constructed a tall, chain-link fence perched above the scoreboard and signage in right field.

If there was anyone else in the crowd rooting for the Phillies, Clay didn't spot him. Nor did Clay stand out. He watched the game but only a few times did he respond to the action. At one point a man next to him asked if he was okay. "This game's a doozy, Pal. You look like somebody died in the family?"

"I just have some things on my mind," Clay said.

It was a game worth the price of admission, inflated or not. Both Roberts for Philadelphia and Newcombe for Brooklyn were vying for their twentieth win. In the case of Roberts, it was his seventh chance at it, his previous attempts marred by bad luck and his team's poor hitting. It was also his fourth start in a week, but on this day, Roberts was the sharper of the two pitchers, although not by much. The Phillies pushed across a run in the fifth on a single by Jones. An inning later, Pee Wee Reese tied it up for the Dodgers when he hit a fly to the short wall in right. It hit the top of the fence and the backspin caused it to balance on the ledge. Reese circled the bases while Ennis could do nothing but look up and wait for a ball that never came down. It just sat there the rest of the day.

The score remained tied until the bottom of the ninth, when Abrams led off with a walk against Roberts. After failing to bunt him over, Reese lined a single to center, bringing up Snider who everybody expected to bunt the winning run to third. Instead, he cracked the first pitch into center for a clear single that looked like it would be the winning hit, especially because the Phillies' centerfielder, Ashburn, possessed a notoriously weak arm. But Ashburn was quick and sure-handed. He ran hard to the infield to cut down the distance, and easily threw out Abrams at the plate. Philadelphia's situation remained dire, but that was the break Roberts needed to work out of the jam. The Phillies won it in the tenth to take the National League pennant.

Although he had been pulling for the Phillies, Clay must have looked as downcast as the rest of the fans shuffling down the narrow gangways that led out of Ebbets Field. "Cheer up, mister," one woman whispered. "There's always next year."

Clay took the train back to Philly, as would the ball club later. At the North Philadelphia Pennsylvania Railroad station a large crowd was already forming to greet the Phillies on their return. Even more people were waiting at Thirtieth Street Station where Clay departed. The entire city had been celebrating since the game had ended. City Hall Square was crowded with revelers. String bands were marching through neighborhoods. Firecrackers left over from Independence Day were exploding. Everybody at the train station it seemed was talking about the game: Reese's crazy homerun, Ashburn's throw, Sisler's game-winning homer, and Robbie's heart. Clay pushed his way through the crowd to a phone booth. Closing the door did little to reduce the din. He slipped a coin in the pay phone and dialed a number.

"It's White." Clay placed a hand over his opposite ear to cut down on the noise. "I need to meet you at the store tonight... No it can't wait. . . An hour's good. I'll see you then."

Clay had just enough time to make his way through the crowded streets to his office to wash up. And fetch a gun.

32

After taking a look at the body, young Pembroke entered the main area of the junior suite, hardly looking distraught.

"The guy should have kept his nose out," Pembroke said. "I knew Barrett all my life. Even when I was little I knew something was wrong with him. It's a wonder he stayed out of prison."

"Sounds like you're the ideal choice to deliver his eulogy," Phyllis said.

"To what, an empty room? No one will miss him. Hell, no one will miss me. Isn't that right, Vivian?"

"You're still my friend, Tom."

"But that's about it, right?"

"The police are going to be here any minute," Phyllis said. "Perhaps we should focus on what we're going to tell them."

"What's he been saying?" Pembroke nodded in the direction of Clay in the Lazy Boy.

"He doesn't know what happened."

"Yo! Clay! Do you remember anything?"

"I remember everything. That's the problem."

"You don't happen to remember killing anybody, do you?"

Clay gave the question some thought. What came to mind was a bar, thick with cigar and cigarette smoke. Clay and Johnny had repaired there to catch up. Johnny said that after leaving the service he had knocked around and eventually decided to come to Pennsylvania to look up his old childhood pals. Nobody in town remembered him, which was to be expected since he hadn't lived there very long, but he was surprised to learn that no one seemed to know much about Clay's whereabouts. After all, he was the minister's kid.

"Word around town is you're dead. Murdered in a stickup in Seattle. Or maybe Sacramento," Johnny said. "As for Chuck, there's a little less certainty."

Most people didn't even remember Chuck, but the barber told Johnny that Chuck had passed through a couple years ago asking about Clay and left after everybody told him Clay was dead. The barber had Chuck's card stuck under the frame of a mirror because he mentioned to Chuck that he had a problem in Philly that needed dealing with.

"He gave me the card, and so here I am. And so are you," Johnny said. "But no Chuck. It was kind of hard to believe, Chuck's a private eye, but you never know how things are going to turn out in life. Where's he at, anyway?"

Clay told Johnny all about Chuck's depression or whatever it was, and how he worried that their friend was more than likely dead or in some asylum. In either case, Clay said that he had a feeling that they'd never see Chuck again.

"He was just broken."

"What about you?" Johnny asked. "How come nobody knows you back home?"

Clay confessed he had gone CO and been disowned by his parents. He told Johnny how he ran into Chuck after the war and turned into Miles Archer.

"Sam Spade's partner?"

"Thank you! Finally someone gets the joke."

"Everyone thinks you're Miles Archer?"

"You're the first person who called me Clay in I don't know how long. Maybe I should just change the name on my driver's license. So where'd you get to after you left that day with your dad?"

"California. But don't change the subject. You're the one with the interesting life."

Johnny asked question after question. Clay had to admit, it felt good to talk about himself. They got something to eat and then drove to a roadhouse outside of town to have drinks and continue the conversation. Finally Clay asked, "Are you going to write a book about me or something?"

"I'm just curious, that's all."

"You should read my letters."

"What letters?"

"You're going to think it's crazy. It is crazy."

Clay told Johnny all about the letters he wrote to his father and never sent when he was a CO. How he practically covered his entire life, including everything he and Johnny and Chuck had done together.

"He should have wrote you back," Johnny said.

"But that's not the weird part. You want another drink?"

"Sure," Johnny beckoned for service. "What's the weird part?"

"The weird part is I started writing to him again after I knew he was dead."

"Why'd you do that?"

"I don't know," Clay said. "Maybe to remind myself who I am. But what about you, Johnny? Come on, tell me. What did you and your Dad do after you went to California?"

"We got on a boat."

"A boat?"

"Let's just get a bottle for a drive. I need some fresh air."

"What kind of boat?"

"It was a tramp steamer actually. Let's blow. I'll tell you more in the car."

Johnny, who had not been drinking as much as Clay and held his liquor better, did the driving with Clay slumped on the passenger's side.

"Okay, so why'd you take a steamer?" Clay asked when they pulled onto a gravel road.

"Because it was headed in the right direction. Let me ask you something, Clay."

"No. No. I'm sick of talking about me. Now we're talking about you."

"This is about me. Seriously. Do you remember the day I left?"

"Sure."

"It was at a baseball game, right? The biggest game of the year. It was all tied up in the last inning when I came to bat and my dad showed up."

"I remember. All of a sudden he just whisked you away. That's a funny word. Whisk."

"So who won the game?"

"Whisk!"

Johnny slowed down and turned into an opening between trees, bringing the car to a stop and throwing it into neutral. "Did our team win the game? Do you remember if we won?"

"Who cares?"

"I do. I've wanted to know for years."

"I really don't remember."

"Think." He turned off the headlights.

"I don't remember. It doesn't matter."

"Well, it mattered to me. It still does."

"Why?"

"It matters to me!"

"Okay, whatever you say. But I don't remember."

"You sure?"

"Why should I remember?"

"So, you really want to know where that steamer took me and my Dad? It took us to Vladivostok."

"Where the hell's that?"

"It's the largest port city in the Soviet Union."

"Why'd you go there?"

"You remember my Dad was a big labor guy. The dope. He thought the Soviet Union was some kind of paradise. Too bad he never bothered to learn Russian. I guess he was just a guy who enjoyed not fitting in."

"He defected?"

273

"We defected. I grew up there. And unlike my dad, I learned the language. I learned how to get along. I learned how to be useful, and trust me, being born in the states, perfectly fluent in English, I was a prized commodity. They groomed me for years."

"Groom you for what?"

"What do you think? To be a translator? They landed me in Mexico by sub, and then I crossed the border into San Diego. I lived there for a year or so, making a background for myself. I was a Bible salesman. Good excuse to travel around. And then they decided they needed me to do something else. I guess I was disposable after all. But the whole time I never could shake this thing. You sure you don't remember who won the game?"

"I told you I don't."

"That's too bad. It means a lot to me. More than the Mother Country. God, how I hate the fucking Soviets. Finally, I just said the hell with it. I defected again. But this time I defected to myself."

"So you don't want to work for them anymore? Can you just quit like that?"

"I didn't actually leave a letter of resignation. They're probably looking for me right now. It's frowned upon to walk."

"So what are you going to do?"

"Go underground. Find a new identity. Hell, I have the training and everything I need to make fake IDs or a driver's license. Remember those letters you told me about?"

"To my dad?"

"Where do you keep them?"

"In my desk at the office. Why?"

"Just good to know," Johnny said. "You're sure you don't know who won the game?"

"I told you, I don't."

"That's too bad. That's really too bad." Johnny reached out, clutched Clay by the lapel of his jacket, wrapped an arm around his head, and quickly snapped his neck. Johnny circled around the car to pull the body onto the ground, remove Clay's wallet and keys, and then dragged him a few feet away and covered him with some leaves.

The next day, Johnny used Clay's keys to enter Chuck's office. He found the bundles of letters in Clay's desk and began reading them. Two hours later, the phone rang. Johnny ignored it, but it continued to ring. Finally Johnny answered the phone. It was a guy named Stoller on the other end of the line. He needed a discreet operative for a private matter.

"Is Chuck available? I heard he's good."

"I'm sorry, but Chuck is out of town."

"Does he have an associate?"

"As a matter of fact, he does. Me."

"So what's your name?"

"The name's Clay White. What's your address?"

Johnny took down the information and as he walked to the door there was a knock. It was the telephone man, come for the phone. Johnny told him not to bother. The office wasn't going out of business after all.

"Yo, Clay!" Tom Pembroke waved a hand in front of Clay's face to catch his attention. "Come on, man, did you shoot Barrett or not?"

"He's too mixed up. He'll never even stand trial," Ryan said.

"But then what happens to him?" Vivian asked.

"I doubt he'll be living at home anymore."

"It was an accident."

"There are no accidents." Clay slowly pushed himself up from his seat. "I asked you all here for a reason."

"Oh my God, he thinks he's in a movie," Phyllis said. "Vivian, please get him to sit down."

"Grandpa, you're getting yourself excited."

Clay turned his attention to Ryan. "You had the most to gain, so naturally I had my concerns about you. The one-armed man. Quick to take offense. Quick to kill. You told me once that there's only one mystery."

"Did I?" Ryan said.

"'What's in it for me,' you said. So what was in it for you?"

"Not enough. Only a desperate man would do something like this. Or someone who lost his sense of . . . balance. My claims on HCA are rock solid. I'm far from desperate."

"Why are you indulging him, dear?" Phyllis said.

"Then there's the dish." Clay looked at Vivian.

"Please sit down, Grandpa."

"Always dropping hints. If something were to happen. If only things were different. You're brave. You're strong. You can spare me some of that courage and strength, surely."

"You're breaking my heart, Grandpa."

"You're good. It's chiefly your eyes, I think, and that throb you get in your voice."

"You're putting on quite a show, Clay," Pembroke said.

"Then there's the gunsel."

"Oh, is it my turn now?"

"Thinks he's tough, but he's just a flunky. Let's make him the fall guy. After all, he did shoot Thursby."

"Who? Clay, you don't even know my name, that's how far gone you are."

"I know your name."

"Okay, what is it?"

"That's enough," Vivian said.

"Don't help him. What's my name? If you're such a great detective, what's my fucking name?"

"It's . . . Nicky."

"Oh, Jesus."

"Little Nicky. I saw you shoot Ellis."

"What about Thursby? Who the hell is Ellis? This is crazy."

"Of course you hit the wrong target. All for the sake of a dame that dumped you after you messed up. You thought you were going to be a hero. You thought she'd be so grateful that you took the initiative and bumped off the guy who hurt her feelings. But you're a loose cannon. Everyone could see that. You were bad for the family business so eventually they banished you to the dead waters of Atlantic City."

"What does Atlantic City have to do with anything?"

"You scraped by for years plying the petty rackets. Then casino gambling came to town and you found yourself sitting pretty and killed your way to the top."

"That sounds like me. You're on a roll, Clay."

"Grandpa, please sit down. I know you want to understand what happened, but it's just too much for you."

"We don't have anything better to do. Let him finish," Pembroke said. "What about Phyllis. You haven't said anything about Phyllis."

"You really are an absolute ass, Tom." Phyllis, sitting on the edge of the bed, recrossed her legs.

Clay turned his attention to Phyllis, who was inspecting her hands as she opened and closed them, stretching the fingers. He stepped forward and stood in front of her. She kept her eyes on her hands, creased and spotted with age. He said nothing, just waited. Finally she glanced up and smiled. "Yes? Was there something?"

"One word."

"One word?"

"One word."

"And what would that be?"

"Bettendorf." In an instant all of the color left her cheeks.

33

Pembroke gripped Clay by the arms and gently pushed him down in the easy chair.

"Take it easy, Mr. White. Time to chill. We have to stick to the subject. What happened to Barrett? You shot him, right? You must have, right?"

"Leave him alone, Tom," Vivian said. "You're not helping."

"I'm just saying."

Had Clay shot Barrett? Had he shot anybody? The faint smell of sulfur in the air triggered a memory. A memory of a night in 1950. A night the city of Philadelphia would not soon forget. The Phillies were on their way to the World Series for the first time in thirty-five years. The streets were still crowded with revelers when Clay arrived outside of Stoller's closed store. He bet a kid with a slingshot a buck he couldn't put out the streetlight in front of the store entrance. One shot did the trick, Clay paid out the wager, and blended in with the crowd banging their pots and pans with ladles and spoons and blowing whistles. After waiting a few minutes, he spotted Stoller unlocking the door to his store and entering. Clay joined a snake dance that was weaving its way past the store and slipped away near the entrance. A string of firecrackers thrown on the street erupted, and while people scattered, kids cheered, and ladies shrieked, Clay opened the door and quickly entered Stoller's store.

A few minutes later, two sharp explosions cracked the air, but no one paid any mind. The only thing that mattered was beating the Yankees in the World Series that was to begin at Shibe Park on Wednesday. A flask was being passed among some men on the street. After Clay left Stoller's shop, he took a sip and passed on the bottle before working his way through the crowd to where he parked his car. He then drove to North Philadelphia and made a brief stop, laying a watch and a gold wedding band on the pavement.

Forty minutes later Clay was breaking the tragic news to Lynne. She fell to her knees, stunned. "It can't be true."

"Save it for the second show." Clay walked to the bar to pour them both a drink.

Slowly she composed herself. "Oh, Clay. You didn't. Did you?"

He held out a drink. "Sometimes wishes do come true."

"I know sometimes I say things."

"I don't have time for this. We're in it together. For the long haul. I'm going to keep my distance for a while, but I'll be back. And don't think about dealing a second hand. It's over between you and Monty no matter what. It's strictly me and you now."

"I know." She rose to her feet and accepted the drink.

"I guess I don't have to tell you to act surprised when you hear the news. Can you handle that end of it?"

"I think so."

"I have to go." He put down his drink, pulled her close, and kissed her.

"I don't even know you," she said.

"You know me now."

The next day a pawn shop reported a couple of negro teenagers were trying to sell a watch and a ring previously owned by a murder victim, a guy named Stoller. There was no other evidence to connect them to the killing, but the district attorney didn't bother launching an investigation. It didn't matter. The boys soon confessed to the crime and pled guilty to manslaughter. They said all they wanted was the money in the guy's wallet and his jewelry. They never intended to kill him, but he resisted.

Two months later, Stoller's widow remarried. She sold his house and business interests and moved to an estate she and her new husband bought in Lower Merion. They hired help and joined the Merion Country Club. They participated in all the Main Line charity functions, and were known to be quite generous with both their time and money. She was especially active. He was a bit reclusive and avoided having his picture land on the society pages of the local papers, but he still became a respected member of the community. He was invited to join the board of several corporations, including the Hosiery Club of America. He could be counted on by management to vote the right way. The smart way. The Philadelphia way.

* * *

"Please Tom, just sit down and wait for the police with the rest of us," Vivian said. She looked like Clay's wife, but Clay knew she had died years ago. He was beginning to put it all together now. He looked at his notes. Box top. Snake Alley. HCA. It was all like a sand castle blown apart by the wind. Only in reverse. It was all starting to come together.

Earlier that night, Vivian, his granddaughter, had dropped by for a visit, giving his caregiver a night off. They watched a Phillies' game together. He had called her Lynne more than once, but now he was clear on things. While watching the game, he had become besieged by the image of Chico Ruiz's twitching leg back in '64. Then Clay had a vision of Chico's face, smiling like a brigand with a pair of gold crowns. Not only did he smile, he spoke to Clay.

"Still need to know who won the game, kid?"

"Yes."

"No es importante."

"It is to me."

"Win, lose. Who gives a fuck?"

"You should have never stolen home. It wasn't worth the gamble."

"True, but Chico look good. So good. Surprise everybody. That Chico, crazy kid. Crazy good."

"What about winning the game? That's what matters."

"No, no, no. Look good. Live fast. Die young."

"Grandpa, are you okay?" asked Vivian. "Maybe we should turn this off. I think it's upsetting you."

It was upsetting him. Memories and regrets assaulted Clay. As always, he allowed the memories to crash together to become one indistinguishable flood. His way to cope. Clay now only experienced scattered moments of the present, like trying to write a letter by lightning flashes. There was Vivian talking on her mobile phone. Then she was saying she had to go. She needed to meet someone to straighten out some business. She wrote down the address of where she was going if there was an emergency. His caregiver was on her way over to watch him, so Clay was supposed to just stay put. The next thing Clay recognized was a hand on his shoulder that shook him until he looked up. A voice was asking where Vivian had gone. He saw a hand pick up the note with the address Vivian had left just in case. The next thing Clay knew he felt pressure on his arm and he was on his feet. He was in a car. He saw street lights flash by. He heard the Beatles on the radio. *Your lips are moving, I cannot hear, Your voice is soothing, But the words aren't clear.* He heard the sound of his steps on a sidewalk then echo in an empty stairwell. He found himself standing in front of a door that was answered by a man who wanted to know why Clay was standing there. Someone else brushed past Clay and into the room, knocking down the man who had answered the door. Clay was pulled inside, and while someone argued, he closed his eyes and tried to banish Chico Ruiz from his brain. "You lose, I win," the Cuban kept saying over and over. "You lose, I win."

There was a loud noise that startled Clay. Chico Ruiz was gone, and with him the torrent of memories. Everything was suddenly quiet. Not quiet at night in the city when there was a siren in the distance or quiet in the country in the winter when the wind lifted tree branches. No, absolute quiet. Soundproof booth quiet. The lack of sound drew more attention to a pungent odor that began to fill the air. Clay opened his eyes and looked down at a pistol in his hand, pale blue smoke drifting from the barrel. At his feet was the man who had answered the door. His blood was pooling on a bathroom floor. *You don't look different, But you have changed, I'm looking through you, You're not the same.*

Clay's mind was suddenly calm, but he was far from certain of his circumstances. He opened his hand to look at the cross-hatch grip on a pistol. "I don't understand," he said to the pistol as much as to himself.

"What don't you understand?" Pembroke asked.

"Would you please leave him alone, Tom."

"I'm sorry. I just keep hoping he'll say something."

"He has nothing to say." Phyllis opened her purse and removed a compact to freshen her makeup while they waited for the police.

"Bettendorf," Clay said.

"See," Tom said. "He does have something to say. It doesn't make any sense, but he has something to say."

"Bettendorf."

"Is that supposed to mean anything at all?"

"Ask her." Clay looked at Phyllis, again gaining his feet.

Phyllis continued to peer at her image in the compact, dabbing rouge on her cheeks. "Vivian, will you please ask your grandfather to stay seated and remain quiet?"

"No, I want to hear this," Pembroke said. "Tell us all about Phyllis."

"We're all tired, Tom."

"Maybe I could say a few things about Phyllis myself."

"Will you kindly shut up?"

"I'm not sure HCA means as much to your husband as it does to you," Pembroke said. "I'm not sure he wouldn't be just as happy to walk away and forget all about stockings and romance novels. I think you think this company is rightfully yours. I think you're the one pushing this whole thing. Hell, I know it. She's been trying to get me to get you to fold, Vivian. Did you know that?"

"I said no such thing."

"Of course Phyllis never says anything directly. She's too smart for that. But she manipulates all the same."

"I'm a regular Lady Macbeth. Thank you for your entertaining insights, Tom. I'm sure all that thinking has overtaxed your system. Perhaps you should rest now."

"It's your fault the guy's dead in there."

"Now you're becoming tiresome."

"He's dead because you had to own HCA. Why is it so important to you? What about that stupid company is so special that you'd do anything to get it? I mean, how old are you? How long have you been angling to get your way on this? Half a century? Won't you ever quit? God knows what you've done all these years to get your hands on a panty hose company."

"And God knows what you've done to get what you want, Tom. And what exactly is it you want? To do nothing. To indulge yourself endlessly without having to work for it. And in order to do nothing you will do anything. You looked at Steve Hess and you saw someone who had all the money you needed, he had the woman you wanted, and you felt all of that was rightfully yours because why? You're a Pembroke? There hasn't been any real money in your family for at least two generations, yet the sense of entitlement never ceases. Desire without the means is all you inherited. And Steve, an adopted child no less, falls into the life that yours should have been. And he lords over you! Of course, you would imagine ways that an accident might occur to your friend, an accident that would allow you to marry his widow and take the fortune that, in your mind, he stole from you."

"Oh, and who might plant the seed for that idea?"

"And then an accident did occur. A real accident," Clay said. "And that changed everything."

"Oh, my god," Phyllis said. "Would someone please keep them both quiet."

"Bettendorf."

"I mean, where are the police when you need them?"

"Stoller was your brother," Clay announced. "You split up after the farming accident in Bettendorf. But when things weren't going so well in L.A. after the war, you tracked him down in Philly. It was more than convenient since your husband found a job with his old Army pal at HCA. The gunsel's right. You had to have that company no matter what."

"We're leaving." Phyllis uncrossed her legs to go, but Ryan laid his hand on her arm and held her down.

"We can't leave. This has become a police matter."

"Did she ever tell you about Bettendorf, Ryan? Did she ever tell you about her father? And her brother? And what they did to her? And that child of a friend that she took in? Did you really buy that yarn, a private op like you? Did it ever occur to you that Lynne really was her daughter?"

"What do you think?"

"Of course you knew. And you looked the other way. You looked the other way when she married the girl to Stoller to get a grip on his dough. Everybody pretending they didn't know each other. Everybody pretending that the guy's bride wasn't really his niece. Or was she his sister? Maybe it was even better than that."

"Shut your mouth!"

Phyllis freed herself from Ryan's grip and lunged at Clay, striking him on the chest with a fist like she was plunging a dagger into his heart. Staggered, he fell to one knee while Pembroke restrained Phyllis and pulled her back on the bed.

Clay could feel the memories, the regrets, beginning to stir, gathering force, but he fought to keep them in check. He knew he only needed to hold on for a few more moments. Vivian knelt beside him, but he pulled off her hand and slowly got to his knees.

"Bettendorf," he said. "That's what it all comes down to. Because of what happened to you back there, back then, you were owed something. Something big. And you were going to take it, no matter what. Even if it was just a stocking company. You thought Stoller would lend your husband the money to pay for the land for a new plant and buy into the company, but he cut you out instead. And that's when the blackmail notes started to arrive. Bettendorf. That was all you needed to write to make Stoller nervous and wonder if his business partner was onto him. And you wrote to Hess and you threatened Bill Ellis, and when that failed you dug up dirt on his brother to stop that plant from being built. And you took up with Nicky. You even wrote a blackmail note to yourself. I bet you thought that was smart."

"I didn't kill my brother," Phyllis said.

"I know you didn't…I did. I shot Stoller."

"You killed him?" Ryan asked.

"You didn't know? You didn't wonder? You didn't ask who had the most to gain?"

"He doesn't know what he's saying." Vivian laid a hand on Clay's shoulder.

"He knows exactly what he's saying," Pembroke said.

"I never wanted any of this." Clay struggled to remain lucid. "I never wanted to lose my mother. I never wanted to go away. I never wanted to come back. But once I had to come back, I only wanted one thing. One simple thing."

"We all want to know who killed Barrett. The police will be here any second. Do you know?"

"That's not what I meant."

"Who killed Barrett?"

The regrets swelled, forming a vortex that gathered force. Clay closed his eyes and held on as best he could. He remembered the echo of his shoes in the stairwell. He remembered Barrett answering the door and someone pushing him aside. He remembered Barrett cowering in the hallway, backing towards the bathroom. He remembered a fat pink-filled soda bottle jammed on the end of a pistol, held by a shaky hand.

"I'll leave town. I won't come back. You don't need to do this," Barrett said.

"You'll be back. There's only one way."

The hand on the pistol trembled. Clay remembered that hand, that soft hand of someone who never worked an hour in his life. Three generations of Pembrokes became one person, but it was the latest incarnation that held the gun, young Tom wearing yellow rubber kitchen gloves. And he wasn't up to the job.

"Do it," Clay had said, not sure why he was suddenly so angry, not sure why he cared. "What are you waiting for?"

"I can't," said Pembroke. "I'm not like you, Clay."

Clay pulled the gun from Pembroke's hand and quickly pulled the trigger, sending a round through the plastic bottle filled with insulation.

Clay didn't see Barrett fall. Pembroke's attempt to make a silencer was far from ideal. It muffled some of the sound, but the report was still loud enough to stun Clay. He dropped the gun. Dazed, he watched the silencer roll on the ground. In a panic, Pembroke tossed the smoking soda bottle into the closet, then pressed the pistol in Clay's hand and hurried out of the room. A few moments later Clay came around, looked at the warm gun in his hand, and wondered what had happened.

"Do you know who killed Barrett?" Ryan asked.

Clay didn't respond. Three killings had folded into one murder. Three became one.

There was an insistent rap on the door, and a voice announced the arrival of the police. Pembroke unlocked the door and a pair of uniformed Philadelphia cops entered the room. Officers Ruiz and Mauch. They were shown the body, and they made a call on the radio. The officers entered the main room and Ruiz asked, "Does anybody know what happened here?"

The only answer anyone offered was to look at Clay.

"So, what's going on?" Mauch stepped forward, gripping the radio piece pinned to his shoulder. "Talk to me, buddy."

"All I know is what I can't remember," Clay said.

ABOUT THE AUTHOR:

Born in Philadelphia, Ed Dinger lives with his family in the Riverdale section of The Bronx, New York. He is a graduate of the Iowa Writers' Workshop, as well as Penn State University and the University of Missouri-Columbia.

ACKNOWLEDGEMENTS:

Thanks to Jon Silbersack for his early valuable insights and Garrett Cook for being the first person to actually read a complete draft and recommending the book to David Osborne. Also thanks are due to David for assigning Alan M. Clark as my editor. Finally, thanks to Alan for serving as my eyes when I could no longer see.

AVAILABLE FROM BROKEN RIVER BOOKS

Death Don't Have No Mercy by William Boyle
Scores by Robert Paul Moreira
The Blind Alley by Jake Hinkson
Will the Sun Ever Come Out Again? by Nate Southard
Visions by Troy James Weaver
The Principle by J David Osborne
Our Love Will Go The Way Of The Salmon by Cameron Pierce
The Last Projector by David James Keaton
Jungle Horses by Scott Adlerberg
Leprechaun in the Hood: The Musical: A Novel by Cameron
Pierce, Adam Cesare, and Shane McKenzie
Long Lost Dog Of It by Michael Kazepis
The Fix by Steve Lowe
Repo Shark by Cody Goodfellow
Incarnations by Chris Deal
Our Blood In Its Blind Circuit by J David Osborne
The First One You Expect by Adam Cesare
XXX Shamus by Red Hammond
Gravesend by William Boyle
Street Raised by Pearce Hansen
Peckerwood by Jedidiah Ayres
The Least of My Scars by Stephen Graham Jones

AVAILABLE FROM LADYBOX BOOKS

The Pulse between Dimensions and the Desert
by Rios de la Luz
Jigsaw Youth by Tiffany Scandal

AVAILABLE FROM KING SHOT PRESS

Leverage by Eric Nelson
Strategies Against Nature by Cody Goodfellow
Killer &Victim by Chris Lambert

Made in the USA
San Bernardino, CA
11 September 2015